PRACTICAL SOCIAL SKILLS FOR AUTISM SPECTRUM DISORDERS

A Norton Professional Book

PRACTICAL SOCIAL SKILLS FOR AUTISM SPECTRUM DISORDERS

DESIGNING CHILD-SPECIFIC INTERVENTIONS

KATHLEEN KOENIG

Foreword by Fred R. Volkmar

W. W. Norton & Company
New York • London

For information about permission to reproduce selections from this book, write to
Permissions, W. W. Norton & Company, Inc., 500 Fifth Avenue, New York, NY 10110

For information about special discounts for bulk purchases, please contact
W. W. Norton Special Sales at specialsales@wwnorton.com or 800-233-4830

Manufacturing by R.R. Donnelley, Harrisonburg
Book design by Bytheway Publishing Services
Production manager: Leeann Graham

Library of Congress Cataloging-in-Publication Data
Koenig, Kathleen.
    Practical social skills for autism spectrum disorders : designing child-specific
interventions / Kathleen Koenig ; foreword by Fred R. Volkmar. — 1st ed.
        p. cm. — (A Norton professional book)
    Includes bibliographical references and index.
    ISBN 978-0-393-70698-7 (hardcover)
    1. Autistic children—Rehabilitation.   2. Social skills in children.   I. Title.
    RJ506.A9K6375 2012
    618.92'85882   dc23   2011041451

ISBN: 978-0-393-70698-7

W. W. Norton & Company, Inc., 500 Fifth Avenue, New York, N.Y. 10110
www.wwnorton.com
W. W. Norton & Company Ltd., Castle House, 75/76 Wells Street, London W1T 3QT

1 2 3 4 5 6 7 8 9 0

For Bob, Sam, and Emily

Contents

• •

Acknowledgments

· ·

So many people have taught, helped, and supported me as I worked on this volume; there are truly too many to name. I will do my best.

My thanks and gratitude to the current and former faculty and staff of the Yale Child Study Center, especially Fred Volkmar, Ami Klin, Celine Saulnier, Kasia Chawarska, Leah Booth, Kathy Tsatsanis, Jamie McPartland, Julie Wolf, Sara Sparrow, Dom Cicchetti, Rhea Paul, Pam Ventola, Larry Scahill, Andrés Martin, Karyn Bailey, Bob Schultz, Kyle Pruett, Phyllis Cohen, Denis Sukhodolsky, Tammy Babitz, Lori Klein, Liz Schoen, Moira Lewis, Monika Lau, Stephanie Maynard, Emily Hau, Wendy Marans, and Stephanie Myles Orleski; each has been a teacher, mentor, and friend.

Thank you to my many colleagues working with and on behalf of children on the autism spectrum, especially Connie Kasari, Nancy Moss, Michael Powers, Jim Loomis, Rosalie Greenbaum, Lois Rosenwald, Deirdre Peterson, Jim Martin, Fred Rapczynski, Ruth Eren, and Susan Williams White.

Finally, a big thank you to Andrea Costella Dawson and Vani Kannan, two thoughtful and patient editors who provided all the support and encouragement I needed.

Foreword

· ·

Since the first description of the syndrome of infantile autism (Kanner, 1943) difficulties in the area of social development and interaction have consistently been identified as a, if not *the*, core vulnerability in autism (Carter, Davis, Klin, & Volkmar, 2005). Social impairments consistently emerge as some of the strongest predictors of diagnosis and prognosis (Siegel, Vukicevic, Elliott, & Kraemer, 1989). Over the last decade it has become increasingly clear that these early social vulnerabilities set the stage for a wide range of later learning problems with very serious impact on the child's overall development and adaptation.

Until recently, interventions to promote social development in children with autism spectrum disorders have been less systematically studied than other aspects of autism; this, in part, has reflected a lack of a sufficient research base for understanding etiology. However, research has now begun to clarify the brain basis of some of the social difficulties observed (Kaiser et al., 2010; Schultz et al., 2000). Further, work from our Center has suggested that when viewing social scenes individuals with autism/Asperger's disorder may miss a majority of the social-emotional cues given their difficulties in processing social information (Klin, Jones, Schultz, Volkmar, & Cohen, 2002). These difficulties emerge very early in life and pose substantial challenges for children on the autism spectrum. Over time, the social impairment is compounded as children with autism spectrum disorders continue to miss important social and contextual information that would inform social understanding. As a result it is not uncommon for teenagers on the spectrum to have social difficulties much like those of preschoolers, in some respects; this, in turn, poses further challenges given the potential for social isolation, teasing, anxiety, and other problems.

Social impairments have increasingly been identified as targets for intervention in recent years. Some of the earliest work in this area occurred within the ABA (applied behavior analysis) approach, which explicitly focused on helping the child learn to develop a shared focus of interest and joint attention with adults (Lovaas & Smith, 1988). Similarly many communication-based programs of intervention also explicitly incorporate a *social*-communication skills teaching component (Tager-Flusberg, Paul, & Lord, 2005). An awareness of the potential for typically developing peers to foster social development in young children with autism has also been emphasized in many model treatment programs (National Research Council, 2001; Strain & Schwartz, 2001) and intervention models have incorporated social goals into overall treatment programs (Rogers et al., 2006).

As a result of this increased interest a variety of social skills intervention programs have been developed over the past decade (Volkmar & Wiesner, 2009). In this regard, this book is timely in describing a number of these approaches that can now be regarded as evidence based; that is, there has been sufficient evidence to show that they work and are "transportable" (Reichow & Volkmar, 2010). These include adult-

mediated teaching (parent/teacher/clinician), group intervention (a hybrid approach with an adult or adults and peers—
either typically developing or having some developmental
difficulty), and peer-mediated approaches (the last used with
preschoolers in particular). Parents, siblings, and other family
members can be especially important in helping children on
the autism spectrum generalize the skills they learn from one
setting to another.

In this volume, my colleague Kathy Koenig describes the
extant research supporting several broad-based approaches
to social intervention as well as a number of evidence-based
strategies for intervention. The careful attention to the range
of strategies and the importance of considering the needs of
the individual child is highlighted, as is the importance of using an integrated approach. Importantly, interventions to promote social development and case examples are presented for
the entire range of children and teens with autism spectrum
disorders, not just those who are verbal or functioning intellectually in the average to above average range.

Beyond learning what best practices and evidence-based
strategies are available to address the needs of children with
autism spectrum disorders, Koenig addresses the issues that
parents and teachers face, as well as the implications of IDEA
2004 for educators. With a wealth of practical and useful information this volume will be profoundly helpful to teachers
and professionals as they consider the needs of the individual child and develop effective interventions to foster social
abilities.

Fred R. Volkmar, MD
Irving B. Harris Professor in the Yale Child Study Center
and Professor of Pediatrics, Psychiatry and Psychology
Yale University School of Medicine

PRACTICAL SOCIAL SKILLS FOR AUTISM SPECTRUM DISORDERS

· ·

CHAPTER ONE

Social Development and Social Disability in Autism Spectrum Disorders

• •

How do we help children or teens with autism spectrum disorder (ASD) lead a life of full engagement with their family and community, with satisfying personal relationships, and an excellent quality of life? This question has parents, educators, clinicians, scientists, and other professionals reading, studying, and testing various approaches as they work with children. Wading through the mountains of information in books, online, and in the media is exhausting and frustrating because there does not seem to be any single, clear way for parents and professionals to proceed. And while this is true, researchers and expert clinicians have made important headway into understanding these disorders in terms of what helps children and what does not. In fact, children can make excellent progress learning new social behaviors, if provided with a comprehensive intervention program. But this cannot be had using a cookbook approach, with the recipe for social success laid out in detailed lessons. Interventionists need a blueprint to guide their own choices for designing intervention for a particular child, and this book aims to be that blueprint.

Promoting social development in children with ASD requires a sophisticated understanding of the social disability as well as a solid grasp of how typical children develop socially. As professionals, we know how to understand and interpret a child's behavior based on what we have learned about children's development from a cognitive point of view. For example, most educators and professionals are familiar with Piaget's stages of cognitive development in children. Piaget's framework helps us understand why babies explore the world through touch, taste, sight, and sound; why preschoolers may fear monsters in a darkened bedroom; why elementary school children focus on rules and have trouble when rules are relaxed; and how abstract reasoning influences behavior in early adolescence and thereafter. We are less familiar with the stages and sequences of social development, although a significant amount of research exists that can enlarge our understanding of children in this domain. Though necessarily incomplete, knowledge of the process of social development, and its interplay with cognitive and temperamental factors as well as the social context, is critical for understanding and intervening with respect to the impairments present in ASD.

Social competency does not develop in isolation from cognitive, emotional, and behavioral development; there is continual interplay among these domains, and competencies in distinct domains may draw from common foundational skills, for example, paying attention or recognizing patterns. One must consider the whole child when planning and implementing intervention; otherwise, intervention is bound to be piecemeal in approach, resulting in gaps in the child's understanding and execution of newly learned skills, as well as haphazard and limited transfer of skills to new contexts.

This chapter describes how ASD is presently defined by mental health professionals and educators to help readers place their understanding of ASD in the practical world of schools and community settings. Many readers will be familiar with these definitions and descriptions. Even more important,

however, is understanding the way social development proceeds in typically developing children and how development
goes awry in children with ASD. For example, a problem with
learning to imitate others has a huge impact on a child's social
and language development. While this seems like a simple
skill, imitation requires cognitive ability and behavioral control, which in turn is linked to emotional regulation. So while
ASD is primarily a social disability, cognitive, emotional, and
behavioral factors play a significant role. Here, I present an
overview of typical social development as well as information
about specific developmental impairments that may occur in
those with ASD. Finally, case examples are presented to bring
to life the children who are the focus of our work, and to demonstrate the complexity of the challenge we face in helping
these children become socially successful.

MENTAL HEALTH AND EDUCATIONAL DEFINITIONS

Autism spectrum disorders, also known as pervasive developmental disorders, are a group of conditions characterized by
developmental impairments in socialization and communication and the presence of restricted and repetitive behaviors
(American Psychiatric Association, 2000; World Health Organization, 1992). Within the current diagnostic classification
system, they include autism, Asperger's disorder, pervasive developmental disorder not otherwise specified (PDD-NOS),
Rett's syndrome, and childhood disintegrative disorder. In the
examples presented throughout the book, ASD denotes the
three most common conditions: autism, Asperger's disorder,
and PDD-NOS, since these are most likely to be the focus of
social learning. Of course, these diagnostic distinctions are
constructs and, in fact, the newest categorization system for
the *Diagnostic and Statistical Manual of Mental Disorders*, the
DSM-V, may not make such fine distinctions. In truth, it is

more important to understand a child based on an individual profile of strengths and impairments rather than a diagnostic label. However, since children in treatment now have been diagnosed according to the *DSM-IV-TR* (American Psychiatric Association, 2000) or the *International Classification of Diseases: Diagnostic Criteria for Research*, 10th ed. (ICD-10; World Health Organization, 1992), these are defined here, followed by some explanation about the changes expected in *DSM-V*, and how that classification system might work.

Autism

Children diagnosed with autism show qualitative impairment in social interaction, manifested by the following:

- Failure to use eye contact, gaze, facial expression, body postures, and gestures to regulate social interaction.
- Failure to develop peer relationships appropriate to developmental level that involve a mutual sharing of interests, activities, and emotions.
- A lack of intentional sharing of positive feelings, interests, or achievements.
- A lack of social or emotional reciprocity as shown by deviant responses to others' emotions, or a lack of modulation of behavior according to social context.

Qualitative impairment in communication includes the following:

- Lack of, or delayed, spoken language that is not accompanied by an attempt to compensate through the use of gestures or alternative means of communication.
- Marked impairment in the ability to initiate or sustain conversational interchange.

4

- Stereotyped and repetitive or idiosyncratic use of words or phrases.
- Lack of varied, spontaneous make-believe or (when young) social imitative play.

In the third domain of impairment, those with autism show restricted, repetitive, and stereotyped patterns of behavior manifested by at least one of the following:

- Encompassing preoccupation with restricted patterns of interest that are abnormal in content or focus, or abnormal in intensity but not content or focus.
- Compulsive adherence to specific, nonfunctional routines or rituals.
- Stereotyped and repetitive motor mannerisms that involve either hand or finger flapping or complex, whole-body movements.
- Preoccupation with parts of objects or nonfunctional aspects of play materials.

Finally, delays or abnormal functioning in social, language, or symbolic, imaginative play have an onset prior to 3 years of age (American Psychiatric Association, 2000; World Health Organization, 1992).

The proposed revision of the *DSM-V* pulls all the diagnoses described above into one category, autism spectrum disorder, with three levels of severity (www.dsm5.org). One reason that this change has been proposed is that children have received different diagnoses from different clinicians at different sites, for both research and clinical purposes. This makes the research hard to interpret, and it certainly does not help the child.

Children with autism may or may not have an intellectual disability (with IQ score <70). For those with an intellectual disability and those who are functioning in the average or above average IQ range, the cognitive profile may show peaks and valleys with regard to verbal or nonverbal skills. Mild or moderate intellectual disability or an uneven pattern of cognitive skills, discussed in Chapter 2, are relevant issues when considering social, communication, and behavioral impairments and subsequent planning for intervention.

From an assessment and intervention point of view, children and adolescents with autism can present in many different ways. The degree of impairment in each domain varies, and family and community factors influence the child's adaptive functioning across settings. We might come across a child who has moderate intellectual disability with inconsistent social interest, weak communication skills, and persistent, nonfunctional motor mannerisms, or, in contrast, a child with superior intellectual functioning, markedly diminished social interest, low average communication skills, and intense interests in unusual topics, such as the subway systems in U.S. cities. Both children would be diagnosed with autism by virtue of impairment in all three domains of functioning and delay noted before the age of 3 years, but clearly they present very differently and would require entirely different approaches to address deficits in social development.

Asperger's Syndrome or Asperger's Disorder

Those diagnosed with Asperger's do not show delays in cognitive or language development and have generally intact formal language skills, for example, age-appropriate receptive and expressive vocabulary, as well as average skills with respect to grammar and syntax (American Psychiatric Association, 2000). The social-communication impairment is manifested by poor conversational skills, an inability to interpret figurative language such as irony and sarcasm, and significant impairment with regard to the use of eye contact, gaze, gestures, and sharing of emotion or experience with others (American Psychiatric Association, 2000; World Health Organization, 1992).

Those with Asperger's disorder have limited insight into the wants, needs, and beliefs of others and tend to interpret behavior quite literally. They may show restricted and repetitive behavior of the same kind as manifested in autism but are more likely to have unusual and intense preoccupations with odd topics (electric fans, road maps, highway signs) and persist in discussing these topics with others, oblivious to the fact that other people do not share their interest. Persons with Asperger's disorder often appear to be talking *at* others rather than *with* them.

Pervasive Developmental Disorder Not Otherwise Specified or Atypical Autism

The diagnostic category of PDD-NOS or atypical autism is used when a child or adolescent shows some symptoms of autism or Asperger's but not enough in terms of number or intensity to warrant the autism or Asperger's diagnosis. As such, this is a diagnostic category in which children's behavioral presentation is tremendously variable. Once again, an individual child's cognitive and behavioral profile is more critical for understanding impairment and planning intervention than is the diagnostic label. Explicit guidelines for obtaining information about this profile are included in Chapter 2. Given the wide variability in symptom domains and the need to view each child as an individual, the most effective intervention takes into account the particular strengths and weaknesses in the domains of social understanding and communication, and the impact these impairments have had over the course of the child's development.

These formal definitions provide good behavioral descriptions of affected individuals, and to some degree provide insight into the challenges these individuals face. But in no way do they give us the full picture of the social world of a child with ASD, as it contrasts with the world of a typically developing child. It is well worth it to understand the intricacies of typical social development to gain insight into the impairments so prominent in those with ASD (Figure 1-1). It is also important to understand that typical children show these social behaviors within a range of time, as some kids are a bit early, some on the later side.

A VERY SHORT HISTORY OF SOCIAL DEVELOPMENT

Infancy

Remarkable as it may seem, newborn babies orient toward the sound of human speech in the first few hours of life (Paul, 2008a). They prefer their mother's voice to that of another and prefer to gaze at faces looking at them in contrast to faces looking in another direction (Jones & Klin, 2008). In the first days of life, a newborn can distinguish his mother's face from that of another woman, based on the contour of the face. Within 3 weeks of life, a newborn will thrust her tongue out in response to an adult modeling this behavior, and by 6 weeks will imitate that same behavior when the model is no longer present (Bishop, Luyster, Richler, & Lord, 2008). These early behaviors provide robust evidence that the newborn is innately "hardwired" to seek and respond to social contact. These preferences for engagement with others lay the foundation for social learning, which continues throughout infancy, childhood, and beyond (Jones & Klin, 2008).

By ages 2 to 3 months, infants begin to scan the environment, attending to stimuli of interest and averting their attention from stimuli that are overly arousing (Calkins & Marcovitch, 2010). This ability to control the level of arousal by turning away from unpleasant environmental stimuli, which re-

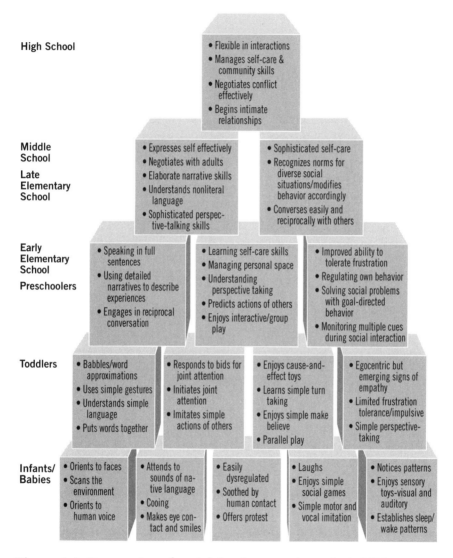

Figure 1-1. Progression of social development in typical children.

quires coordinating attention and motor skills, lays the foundation for self-regulatory skills. Babies learn to distract themselves from distressing stimuli in the environment, whether visual or auditory. Further, they learn to soothe themselves with vocalization and sensory exploration, sometimes of their own hands and feet. Parents support a baby's attempts to self-regulate, using soothing strategies such as repetitive sound or movement (Calkins & Marcovitch, 2010; Lewis & Carpendale, 2009). Babies use cooing, crying, smiling, and frowning to communicate their needs, and parents become acutely attuned to the kinds of cries and sounds the child makes and what these signals mean. The constant association of the parent with food and comfort begins the process by which the child bonds and begins to see human engagement as a rewarding and pleasurable experience. This kind of sensory and emotional synchrony between caregiver and child provides a secure environment for ongoing development, since the child becomes confident that the caregiver will control the environment such that the child will not become overwhelmed with sensory stimulation (Calkins & Marcovitch, 2010).

Imitation behavior continues over the next 3 months of life, and by 6 months of age, children begin to link imitation (their own and other's) with *intentionality*, the idea that people behave with certain intentions in mind (Bishop et al., 2008). Imitation and the concept of intentionality are critical foundations for the development and understanding of social relationships.

Over the course of the first 6 months of life, babies become attuned to the speech sounds native to their environment and become sensitive to the melody of their native language (Paul, 2008a). In this way, they are more attentive to the repetitive sounds and segments of the language that surrounds them, while ignoring sounds and language segments that are less common. Essentially, they tune into sounds that they hear consistently, and parse out sound fragments into discrete words. This attunement to discrete speech sounds is a necessary component of language development, which unfolds in the context of social relationships (Paul, 2008a).

By 6 to 9 months of age, babies engage in social games with caregivers, smiling and cooing in response to caregiver initiation, and signaling for attention of their needs through a variety of vocal and gestural means. Babies begin to babble (using consonant and vowel combinations), and adults reinforce this behavior with imitation and visible excitement. Babies share enjoyment with others through social games such as peek-a-boo. They communicate their enjoyment with smiles, laughter, eye contact, and movement. Children as young as 8 months of age will perceive an expression of concern on an adult's face as a warning signal and will not advance toward a desired object (Cole, Armstrong, & Pemberton, 2010).

Around this same time, babies develop the capacity to share a focus of attention with another, following the gaze of another to an external referent (an object or activity) (Chawarska & Volkmar, 2005). This manifestation of *joint attention* is an important foundation for language learning, since a baby learns to associate a sound (word) with a referent in the environment. Next, a baby learns to initiate a joint attention sequence, using vocalization and gaze to direct the caregiver's attention to an object or activity of interest.

Over time, as a baby understands that the sound she hears, paired with an object that she and her mother are referencing, is the name of that object, language begins to emerge (Paul, 2008a). In these experiences of joint attention, a child not only learns the label for a particular object, person, or activity but also begins to learn to interpret the mother's emotional communication, whether tone of voice, body language, or vocal emphasis on particular syllables or sounds (Carlson, 2009; Cole et al., 2010).

Babbling increases over the course of the first year, and typically developing children are often using single words by 12 months of age. By 18 months children may have 50 or more single words and are beginning to put words together in short phrases (Paul, 2008a). Additionally, babies and toddlers show competency in imitating and responding to facial expressions of others (Jones & Klin, 2008). Children between the ages of 2 and 3 years will perceive the distress of other children; for example, when they observe crying, they may take steps to comfort the distressed person (Litvack-Miller, McDougall, & Romney, 1997). This signals the early signs of empathy, which serves as a foundation for the development of social relationships (Eisenberg et al., 1996).

Toddlers

In the second year of life, children begin to explore cause-and-effect toys and play simple make-believe games, for example, pretending that a banana is a telephone (Chawarska & Volkmar, 2005). They play in parallel with other children and will often observe another child's play, even if they do not attempt to join in. As toddlers, children depend on parents and other caregivers to guide their behavior through explicit instructions and directions. Between the ages of 18 and 30 months, children learn to comply with adult directives (Bibock, Carpendale, & Müller, 2009). At this developmental level, they do not possess the ability to inhibit responses, for example, to delay pursuit of a desired object or control their behavior when angry or upset. Adults provide soothing for children, helping them manage their arousal and agitation (whether happily excited or angry and frustrated). Adults organize the child's world on an environmental level, for example, moving an over-excited child to a less stimulating environment, or on an interpersonal level, using physical contact, such as hugging or carrying the child, to reduce arousal. As children approach preschool age, they begin to develop the ability to inhibit responses and to regulate emotion (Bibock et al., 2009). Inhibition is the ability to delay or not perform a desired behavior in the absence of external monitoring (Karreman, van Tuijl, van Aken, & Dekovic, 2006). For example, a child may follow an adult directive not to take a cookie from a plate while the adult is present (compliance) but not be able to resist when no adult is there to monitor behavior (failure to inhibit). A third important cognitive and behavioral process to come online is the ability to regulate emotion (Carlson, 2009). Children must learn to cope with frustration, manage fear and anxiety, and control behavior when angry. Over the course of the preschool years, from approximately 3 to 5 years of age, children use external support provided by adults to help them internalize these controls (Zelazo, Qu, & Kesek, 2010). Ultimately they develop their own strategies to manage emotion and behavior. Actually, the child's motivation to self-manage is related to his desire to be socially accepted (Carlson, 2009).

Preschool and Kindergarten Students

The ability to take the perspective of another person, that is, to appreciate that others have thoughts, feelings, and beliefs that differ from one's own emerges between the third and fourth year of life (Benson & Sabbagh, 2010). Studies in which children are asked to describe what another might do based on their personal knowledge shows that, by age 3 to 4 years, children can appreciate that other people act based on their own ideas, rather than the ideas of an observer. The ability to understand that other people act based on their perceptions or understanding of a situation versus what is objectively happening is a critical skill for the development of social competency (Benson & Sabbagh, 2010).

At around 3 years of age, children are beginning to narrate their experience in simple terms (Reese, Yan, Jack, & Hayne,

2010). They are able to describe things that are happening or have happened, and thus they are developing an ability to think abstractly about events. Make-believe play facilitates the capacity to represent the world symbolically, a critical skill for all kinds of problem solving. Ultimately, more elaborate pretend play helps children develop templates for organizing their experiences. As children learn more about the social world, in terms of how things happen and why things happen as they do, they develop a sound understanding of social relationships and contingencies.

By preschool, children show strong interest in other children of the same age and begin to engage in social relationships in earnest. Children of this age show preferences for particular children, initiate social contact, and engage in cooperative play. Most important, children use language to communicate their needs and wants, to learn about other adults and children in their environment, and, particularly, to mediate their own behavior (Lewis & Carpendale, 2009; Morrison, Cameron Ponitz, & McClelland, 2010). In other words, children use their words as a way to delay acting impulsively and to guide their behavior in novel situations. Children become increasingly adept at using language to mediate their experience of the environment, which helps develop self-regulation abilities (Loth, 2008). Children of 3 and 4 years of age are often noted talking through the steps of a task, or repeating instructions they have heard as a way to support their behavior (Cole et al., 2010). Further, the greater familiarity children have with the language of emotion, the more they are able to label feeling states and exert control over their behavior.

Once children enter kindergarten, they have likely had some experience interacting in a group situation. Critical social skills at this point are the ability to attend to information and to shift attention, to understand language at the same level as peers, and to show some measure of emotional and behavioral control. Behavioral control, which involves inhibiting impulsive responding, either through distraction or some other means, is critical for skills such as waiting for a turn and taking turns in conversation. By this time children clearly understand that others have different thoughts and feelings, and that others may act on those thoughts and feelings. Social interactions become complex because children need to pay attention to multiple actors in the social environment (Lewis & Carpendale, 2009). Typically developing children show increased ability to solve social problems using goal-directed behavior and planning (Landry, Smith, & Swank, 2009). Over the course of the early elementary school years, children develop the ability to modify their behavior based on their perception of the social context. Once again, the importance of being able to narrate one's own experience is critical for learning how to adapt behavior in a novel situation based on one's understanding of similar past situations.

Elementary School-Age Students

Socially competent elementary school children maintain relationships with peers, make judgments about their behavior and that of others, and act based on those judgments (Landry et al., 2009). They must be flexible in interactions, tolerate frustration, and accommodate others' differences. Further, they interact with adults by complying with adult instructions or negotiating for a different solution or outcome to a problem (Landry et al., 2009). They manage conflict with peers and adults, not in the sense that they do not become upset or frustrated, but in that they are able to handle their own level of distress and regulate their level of arousal or agitation downward to contain their behavior. Early pretend play, in which children practice various roles, helps children learn how to symbolically represent real-life situations and consider various problem-solving scenarios.

Adults play a significant role in helping school-age children develop social competency by providing *scaffolding* of social situations from very early on (Bibock et al., 2009). Scaffolding is defined as actions taken by an adult, whether behavior or conversation, to provide structure and support for children as they engage in social interaction. Scaffolding is effective in helping the child learn how to handle a situation independently when the level of support is appropriate to the child's developmental level, and the timing of the interaction fits the situation (Bibock et al., 2009). If children are given too much freedom for decision making, they can become overwhelmed with options and show poor ability to make prudent choices about behavior. Conversely, children given too little freedom to make decisions in social situations are not challenged to develop an internal set of strategies for social decision making. By the time children leave elementary school, they are expected to be able to function relatively independently with regard to peer relationships, initiating contact, maintaining relationships, and negotiating successfully through conflict. Children who enter middle school without these skills are at a distinct disadvantage, since the social landscape becomes much more complex at that point (Bibock et al., 2009). In fact, competency in social problem solving in middle childhood predicts early adolescent social competence (Landry et al., 2009).

Middle School Students

Preteens and young teens must act on multiple pieces of social information, including an understanding of the broad social context, an understanding of the players in a particular interaction, and knowledge about acceptable and unacceptable behavior related to sex-specific roles (Berndt, Hawkins, & Jiao, 1999). Many of the rules for social behavior are different for boys and girls and are substantially different from what may have been acceptable in elementary school. Appearance and fitting in with the peer group become paramount. In early adolescence (which usually coincides with junior high or late middle school) the importance of cliques and crowds is at its height. Young teens must understand where they fit within their group of friends (their clique) and where the clique fits in the larger school environment (the crowd). To adults, this kind of distinction and fine discrimination may seem a bit absurd, but for the young women and men involved, it feels very important. Those who do not grasp the gestalt of the larger social scene in their grade or in their school miss out on important information that will make a difference as they navigate social interactions throughout the school day and during extracurricular activities.

Conflict with adults increases during the early teen years and decreases as teens develop greater ability to interact effectively with adults (Landry et al., 2009). Competency in interactions with adults is mirrored by competency in interactions with peers to some extent. Adolescents who are able to listen and enjoy positive interactions, to generate multiple solutions to potential problems, and to engage with adults without denial or disruptive behavior are more likely to show social competency (Landry et al., 2009).

High School Students

Young teens who are socially successful have more sophisticated ways of thinking about friendships and friendship-related issues (Barry & Wigfield, 2002). Those who have close mutual friendships have better social-cognitive and behavioral skills than those who do not. Additionally, friendships have emergent properties; that is, expectations and roles within a relationship develop and change over time (Parker & Asher, 1993). Friendships between girls are more intimate than those between boys during the teen years. During adolescence, teens develop an increasing capacity to engage in more intimate relationships with same-sex and opposite-sex friends. Young women move forward more quickly in this process and develop intimate relationships to adult levels by their college years, whereas young men do not develop mature intimate relationships until the early adult years (Reis, Lin, Bennett, & Nezlek, 1993). Failure to develop the personal understanding and skills needed to interact intimately with same-sex and opposite-sex peers during this time results in significant social challenges in the early adult years, when a majority of young adults are seeking an intimate, sexual relationship (Reis et al., 1993).

To summarize, social competency in any individual is built from a myriad of basic and multidimensional skills, and this competency is demonstrated by the fluid application of these skills in a particular social context. A socially competent person assembles needed skills in prearranged or novel ways in order to interact effectively with the environment. The dynamic nature of the process of competent social interaction creates complexity for teaching social skills. In kids with ASD, it is not just the lack of a particular behavior or friendship skill, or knowledge of when the behavior should be applied, but also the absence of a rich narrative history of social experiences and successful social interactions on which to draw when confronting a social situation. The challenge this presents to a person with ASD cannot be overemphasized.

SOCIAL AND COMMUNICATION IMPAIRMENT
IN AUTISM SPECTRUM DISORDERS

If we consider the social skills and competencies of a typically developing child, as well as the neurobiological, behavioral, and developmental deficits present in a child with ASD, we are in a good position to understand how development goes awry. This in turn helps with understanding the implications for working with children to promote social competency.

Children with ASD have neurobiological abnormalities that make them less predisposed to engage in social interaction. Some research has demonstrated that the reward system in the brain, responsible for helping a child link behavior with pleasurable feelings, is weaker in children with ASD than in the typically developing child (Scott-Van Zeeland, Dapretto, Ghahremani, Poldrack, & Bookheimer, 2010). Throughout development, these children are less responsive to the social environment in general and do not benefit from the many implicit social learning experiences available from day to day (Jones & Klin, 2008). For example, if a father praises a typically developing child for a particular behavior, the child feels pleased and is more likely to behave in the same way again. Usually, social reinforcement of this type is quite compelling to children and helps parents and other adults shape behavior. If a child with ASD is less responsive to praise, this impacts his learning and relationships with others.

Early Social Impairment

While typical children show a preference for the human voice, children with ASD do not show this same preference (Paul, 2008a). These children show reduced competency in the perception of faces (identity) and facial expressions. Toddlers with ASD spend as much time looking at nonsocial stimuli as social stimuli, in contrast to typically developing children, who prefer to look at social stimuli. Jones and Klin (2008) suggest that the world of a baby with ASD may be one of "a chaos of sights and sounds." In this sense, the organizing of perceptual experience that takes place in a baby's first year of life, as she is guided by her caregiver's soothing and stimulating interactions, is weak or absent for these children.

Children with ASD tend not to engage in social games (such as peek-a-boo) to the same extent as their typically developing peers and show reduced direct eye contact and ability to follow a gaze or point to something of interest (Chawarska & Volkmar, 2005). This lack of response to joint attention cues impacts language learning. Since these children do not share attention with adults to an object or an activity, they do not learn that the sound (word) they hear is the label for that object or activity (Paul, 2008a). Similarly, toddlers with ASD are not likely to bring a book or toy to a parent to show (initiating joint attention), since they do not experience an internal drive to share experiences (Chawarska & Volkmar, 2005). The lack of initiation of joint attention inhibits the learning of language and learning about the social world. These children become fixated on very concrete aspects of the physical world, such as a toy or object, or on letters or numbers, because these things do not change and are predictable. Repetitive activity may be soothing for a child for whom the world makes little sense. Subsequently, attempts to disrupt repetitive behavior or remove an object or toy that the child has become fixated on can be inordinately stressful for the child, since it may be a point of organization for her world.

Emotion and behavior dysregulation are frequently associated features of the symptom picture in children with ASD. If one considers how behavior regulation develops over the course of a typical child's early life, in the context of the parent-child interaction, and in part due to the child's increased skill at taking the perspective of another, it is easy to see why children with ASD have difficulty with these developmental challenges. Many times, toddlers and preschoolers with ASD have not been able to use their relationship with a caregiver to help manage their emotional reactions and frustration, and thus aggression and self-injury can occur.

The impact of impaired language comprehension and general language competency cannot be overstated. As we have seen, typically developing children use language to mediate their own behavior, for example, to guide themselves in situations where they have been told a rule and need to comply. By 3 years of age, typical children are using their narrative language skills to understand their own experiences and to make sense of novel experiences by making comparisons. Children without narrative language skills, in particular sequencing skills, have little ability to organize their past experiences in memory in such a way that they can draw on these memories to help them understand the present (Loth, 2008). Without this template for understanding, it is clear why children with ASD avoid novel situations and transitions, even to activities they have done many times previously.

A further consequence of the reduced salience of the social environment is that affected children do not learn how to interpret social cues within the environment, such as how facial expressions, gestures, tone of voice, or body language convey information (Koenig, De Los Reyes, Cicchetti, Scahill, & Klin, 2009). The development of empathy, in terms of noting how others behave and inferring feeling states from that behavior, is disrupted, so these children may not show appropriate displays of emotion in context.

Children with ASD may focus on concrete and irrelevant details when attempting to solve a problem because they have difficulty distinguishing what is important to attend to versus what can be disregarded. This presents significant problems for successful social interaction, since understanding the gestalt of a social situation is usually more important than interpreting every detail (Koenig et al., 2009). This taps into organizational skills, which are frequently, but not always, problematic for children with ASD (Tsatsanis, 2005).

Let's take a couple of examples of simple social situations that might occur for a school-age child, to get a sense of the complexity. A typically developing 6-year-old girl enters her first grade classroom for the first time. She sees a circle of child-size chairs on one side of the room and several children sitting on those chairs. Three sets of materials are placed on tables positioned at a distance from one another across the room. No one is using these materials at present. One wall has a set of hooks and cubbies, and the child can see some jackets on hooks and lunchboxes in the cubbies. Children can be seen in the hallway, entering other classrooms, and the child can see a girl from her kindergarten class going into a different classroom. Two adults are in the room, one helping a boy with his jacket, and one who turns to say hello to her with a smile. It seems like a simple scenario, but in fact, this typically developing child must process a good deal of social information about this environment to know what to do next. She must grasp that the adults will take the lead here, that she should respond to the adult who greeted her, that a smile means this adult is friendly and notices her, and that she probably should hang up her coat and stow her lunchbox in a cubby. With a simple directive from the teacher to join the other children, she knows she should sit down in the circle of chairs. She may know to say hello to another child or ask that child's name.

Let's take the same scenario with a 6-year-old girl with autism. She might overfocus on some details, like the painting materials on one table, while failing to note that the other children are not using the materials but sitting in the circle of chairs. She may dart to those materials and begin to manipulate them. She may not notice the teacher's smile or know how to interpret it, and a simple phrase such as "join the other children" might be confusing because although she has learned much language via structured intervention, she does not know what the word *join* means. Further, she cannot infer the meaning of the word from the context. While this little girl may see the other children, she may not note that they are grouped together sitting in a circle (the visual gestalt) and consequently realize that she should do the same (a social expectation). She may see a familiar child from last year and leave the classroom to follow that child down the hall. The routine of an elementary school, in that one is assigned to a particular classroom, may not be something she has been explicitly taught, and so she does not appreciate the need to stay in her new classroom. In this scenario, the child has trouble interpreting facial expressions and language, she does not understand the implicit rules in a classroom, nor does she appreciate any need to conform to a pattern of behavior she observes in her peers. In fact, she does not actually see any such pattern. Her attempts to follow a familiar child or to explore materials that interest her may be misconstrued as willful misbehavior in contrast to a genuine inability to assess her social context in a meaningful way. A seemingly simple situation, in which little interaction with others is required, has multiple requirements and expectations for appropriate social behavior. Failure to behave as expected sets this child apart from peers.

A second example illustrates the complexity of a situation in which a child must interpret a basic social context as well as the behavior of peers. A fifth grade boy diagnosed with Asperger's disorder enters the playground of his school for recess. It is a noisy and confusing setting for him, with six adults and more than 40 children from grades four and five outside at once. He sees groups of children together, some kicking a ball, some climbing on the jungle gym, and some standing by a tree talking. He thinks standing by the tree would be okay, so he walks over, failing to realize that the group under the tree is all girls. Some of these girls he knows and played with in his early elementary school years, and he has not noticed that this year, the girls and boys seem to play separately. He says hello to one girl, who replies but also rolls her eyes, and the other girls laugh. The boy does not understand what her facial gesture means, and he takes the laughter to mean he is welcome. In any case, the girls ignore him, and he cannot seem to follow the conversation. He tries to tell them about his interest in

Japanese anime, talking as loudly as he can to be heard over their voices and laughter. Occasionally one of the girls responds, using sarcasm to convey that the group has little interest in this topic. Ultimately, the girls move away from him, and the recess period ends. Here, the child with Asperger's has no ability to appreciate the changes in social expectations based on sex that have become more prominent as he and his peers approach adolescence. He does not read facial expressions, nor does he interpret the girls' laughter accurately. He does not recognize that he is being ignored, as that would involve integrating information about the girls' body language, facial expressions, and comments. The anime discussion falls flat because he does not perceive that the girls are not interested (he cannot interpret sarcasm), and his attempts to speak as loudly as possible only make him stand out as unusual to his peers. In this situation and the previous example, interacting successfully with others requires a complex set of abilities, which involves accurate perception and interpretation of others' behavior, a good sense of timing, knowledge of social norms, and the ability to take the perspective of another. Clearly these are complicated situations for these children, which require explicit teaching and practice.

One can see from these two examples that a host of skills and complex abilities are needed to navigate the social world. Further, as a child grows and the number of contexts he must navigate is enlarged, the more complex the social demands become. By high school and young adulthood, the number of personal and social skills needed to function, and the need for flexible application of these skills, is paramount. Given this complexity, it is more critical than ever that intervention to address social impairment be customized to the child's particular profile of strengths and weaknesses.

A broad-based understanding of how social development proceeds in typically developing children is needed to effectively intervene with children on the autism spectrum with the goal of helping them become socially competent. Typically developing children are born with a predisposition toward social engagement and begin learning about the social world in the first few days of life. The process of learning about the social environment as one develops physically, cognitively, and emotionally continues throughout childhood, adolescence, and adulthood. By the time children approach adolescence, they are sophisticated partners in social interaction. For the most part, this process of learning about the social world and becoming socially competent happens without explicit teaching from others in the environment. Therein lies the difficulty with helping children with ASD develop social competency. An interventionist must have some understanding of the deficits in "hardwiring" that cause the impairment, as well as the idiosyncratic responses to the environment these children show. Facilitating social development in children with ASD is a process by which children incorporate and integrate new ways of thinking and behaving into their social repertoire. In this regard, the focus of intervention goes far beyond teaching children a discrete set of skills to be applied in social settings.

CHAPTER TWO

Evidence-Based and Best Practices

· ·

Before I begin describing approaches and strategies for promoting social skill development, let's consider why social competency is so important. In many ways, intervention focused on promoting social development is in its infancy, compared with intervention designed to promote language learning or improve self-care skills. In years past, the priority was addressing language impairment and maladaptive behavior in children with ASD, given how severe these problems were, so that helping children learn to interact with peers appropriately seemed less urgent. Fortunately, we have come a long way.

IMPROVING SOCIAL COMPETENCY: WHO, WHAT, AND WHY?

Why address social functioning in children and adolescents with ASD? For the children involved and their families, the answer is obvious: Satisfying social relationships are associated with good psychological and physical health. However, some school personnel and other professionals have raised this question during continuing education workshops and in meetings with parents and community mental health providers. If schools are charged with preparing children to meet their future academically, why should they take on the complex task of promoting social development? In fact, even the most brilliant individual must function socially in the day-to-day world to have a successful career. Buying groceries, making a phone call, following up on an online purchase, taking a bus or train, hailing a taxi, communicating with employers and employees, communicating with police or firefighters if needed, and working successfully with colleagues all require competent social skills. The individual with minimal interest in social interaction for its own sake still lives in a world populated by others, and many times, there is no choice but to interact.

U.S. law and U.S. Department of Education policy recognize this fact. The mission of the U.S. Department of Education is "to promote student achievement and preparation for global competitiveness by fostering educational excellence and ensuring equal access" (http://www2.ed.gov/about/overview/fed/role.html). Obviously, this cannot be achieved if students are unable to work cooperatively with others toward common ends. Competent social skills are necessary to reach this goal. Essentially, schools are responsible for educating children and adolescents so that they can develop the skills and access the tools needed to become productive members of the community and society as a whole. Clearly, these skills go beyond reading, writing, and mathematics. Students must be competent in critical thinking skills, analytic skills, communication skills, and adaptive skills, that is, the skills needed to function independently in the real world.

The relationship between poor academic outcomes and behavioral problems, such as delinquency, teen pregnancy, mental health problems, and substance abuse is well known (Brier, 1995; McEvoy & Welker, 2000). But what do we know about the consequences of poor social functioning? Outcome research on ASD provides some information about how well these individuals do over time, even with strong intellectual and academic skills. While there has been improvement in the last 10 years in the number of individuals functioning independently, the outcomes of the majority of this group are quite poor (Howlin, Mawhood, & Rutter, 2000; Klin et al., 2007). In a sample of 187 children diagnosed with ASD without intellectual disability, interpersonal social functioning, measured by the Vineland Adaptive Behavior Scales Socialization Score, was between 3 and 4 years delayed relative to chronological age (Klin et al., 2007). So a sixth grade student with ASD beginning middle school might have interpersonal skills commensurate with second to third grade students.

Further, average or above-average intellectual functioning and good academic performance do not predict successful adaptive functioning. As children with ASD grow older, the gap between intellectual potential and day-to-day functioning widens (Klin et al., 2007). This is not surprising since the social world becomes more abstract and complex as children grow. School-aged children with ASD are more likely to be isolated and feel lonely compared to typically developing children (Bauminger & Kasari, 2001; Locke, Ishijima, Kasari, & London, 2010; Rothman-Fuller, Kasari, Chamberlain, & Locke, 2010). Additionally, children who are socially disconnected, lonely, and isolated are at greater risk for mental health problems, including depression and anxiety (White, Oswald, Ollendick, & Scahill, 2009; White et al., 2010).

When considering the education of children and adolescents with ASD, we look to the Individuals With Disabilities Education Improvement Act, known as IDEA 2004 (Pub. L. 108-446). The purpose of this statute is to "ensure that all children with disabilities have available to them a free appropriate public education that emphasizes special education and related services designed to meet their unique needs and prepare them for *further education, employment, and independent living*" (italics added). This reauthorization of the Education for All Handicapped Children Act of 1975 (PL 94-142) was deliberately crafted to align with the purpose of the No Child Left Behind Act of 2001, which is to "ensure that all children have a fair, equal, and significant opportunity to obtain a high-quality education and reach, at a minimum, proficiency on challenging state academic achievement standards and state academic assessments." This means that children with disabilities must meet established goals for performance just as nondisabled children do; schools and states must establish procedures for accountability (Wright & Wright, 2007). For detailed information about IDEA 2004, the reader is referred to *Special Education Law* (2nd ed.), by Wright and Wright (2007).

For our purposes, however, the essential point is that schools are responsible not only for promoting success in academic learning but also for "ensuring equality of opportunity, full participation, independent living, and economic self-sufficiency for individuals with disabilities" (20 U.S.C. § 1400 [c]). Additionally, IDEA includes a statute regarding Response to Intervention (RtI) that describes the process and procedures school districts may use for evaluating children to determine whether they have a specific learning disability and to determine what intensity of intervention is needed.

RESPONSE TO INTERVENTION

RtI is a broad-based way to ascertain whether a child has learning needs that require modified instruction. In the past, children were classified as having a learning disability, and therefore requiring special education services, based on documentation of a discrepancy between the child's potential for learning, typically determined by developmental level or IQ score, and the child's mastery of developmental or academic tasks. The RtI model determines that a child needs more focused instruction based on the student's response to the teacher's instruction. If a child makes gains in learning, the instructional strategies are considered successful, and if a child does not make gains, the instructional strategies are considered insufficient. Typically, the RtI process includes three or four tiers of instruction; the first tier including general instruction (based on research findings of efficacy), and the second tier incorporating more differentiated instruction tailored to the child's learning needs (Hale, 2008). A child who is not making progress may require special education services (tier 3), and the requirement is that these services are based on peer-reviewed research. The RtI process does not replace a comprehensive evaluation, and that evaluation as well as RtI may be used to determine whether a child qualifies for special education services.

Once it is determined that the child has such needs, IDEA 2004 requires that instruction for children with disabilities be based on scientifically based research, which is defined by law as

(A) research that involves the application of rigorous, systematic, and objective procedures to obtain reliable and valid knowledge relevant to education activities and programs; and (B) includes research that—(i) employs systematic, empirical methods that draw on observation or experiment; (ii) involves rigorous data analyses that are adequate to test the stated hypotheses and justify the general conclusions drawn; (iii) relies on measurements or observational methods that provide reliable and valid data across evaluators and observers, across multiple measurements and observations, and across studies by the same or different investigators; (iv) is evaluated using experimental or quasi-experimental designs in which individuals, entities, programs, or activities are assigned to different conditions and with appropriate controls to evaluate the effects of the condition of interest, with a preference for random-assignment experiments, or other designs to the extent that those designs contain within-condition or across-condition controls; (v) ensures that experimental studies are presented in sufficient detail and clarity to allow for replication or, at a minimum, offer the opportunity to build systematically on their findings; and (vi) has been accepted by a peer-reviewed journal or approved by a panel of independent experts through a comparably rigorous, objective, and scientific review. (20 U.S.C. 7801 [37])

An interesting caveat is that the law recognizes that in some situations there is scant information on research-based methods for intervention, and that in those situations we may rely on the expertise of professionals. For children with ASD, an important resource with regard to what practices are highly recommended or have some research support is the report by the Committee on Educational Interventions for Children With Autism, titled *Educating Children With Autism* (National Research Council, 2001). This volume includes a section on the characteristics of effective intervention, which provides guidelines for developing intervention to address communication, social, sensory, and motor deficits; delays in adaptive behavior; and problem behavior and cognitive impairment. Chapter 5 provides information on specific strategies for instruction in an individual or group setting.

Many interventions for individuals with ASD are touted in books, in workshops, and on the Internet. Unfortunately, these interventions run the gamut from well established and based on sound research to snake oil and magic. Parents, but also professionals, can be fooled by approaches that seem science based. Professionals working with children with ASD not only must distinguish between approaches and strategies that are research based and those that are not, but may be responsible for helping parents and colleagues make these distinctions. Given the numerous interventions available for children with ASD and the pressure parents and professionals feel to do as much as they can, as quickly as they can, it can be difficult to be the member of the team that challenges a particular idea for intervention. Nonetheless, it may be necessary in order to keep the child's best interests at the forefront of intervention planning.

Another consideration in helping children on the spectrum develop socially is that the approaches and strategies that are effective for training discrete, invariant behaviors (e.g., tying your shoe) may not be as effective when teaching appropriate social behavior. Competent social functioning includes the ability to assess the social context, the participants, and the situation, and to generate appropriate responses with an eye toward communicating effectively and fluidly, with appropriate timing. This kind of behavior requires that individuals think on their feet, so to speak, which is exactly the kind of intuitive thinking that is problematic for those with ASD. This is the crux of the problem of teaching social behavior and, unfortunately, despite the many excellent resources available online and in print focused on helping those with ASD develop social skills, no single curriculum or approach can claim broadbased success.

WHAT DOES EVIDENCE-BASED MEAN?

Essentially, evidence-based practices are those that we know to be effective based on rigorous research. Current research findings in education and psychology related to autism intervention are evaluated using a formal framework that presents a hierarchy of the kind of evidence needed to label an intervention as possibly efficacious, probably efficacious, or efficacious. Case studies and case series may indicate that an intervention is possibly efficacious, but to consider an intervention efficacious, it must be tested with increased standards of rigor, usually in controlled experiments with random assignment of subjects to different intervention conditions. These controlled trials are complex, expensive, and time consuming, which presents a problem since the goal is to intervene early and intensively with children to have the best chance of success. Children, families, and interventionists need information about what works now. Further, sometimes evidence-based approaches require specialized knowledge or training on the part of the interventionist, and professionals, despite a strong commitment to intervene effectively, do not have this knowledge or training. When there is a gap between what a child needs and the available evidence-based interventions, professionals can look to best practices for guidance. Best practices are intervention approaches and strategies that are based on a solid theoretical understanding of the challenges these children face and the kinds of intervention approaches that have some evidence of effectiveness, even if the evidence is not currently strong enough to allow the approach to be considered efficacious (National Research Council, 2001). Best practices have been identified as those that have the endorsement of experts in the field and incorporate aspects of evidence-based approaches as well. In any case, matching the child's developmental level, behavioral characteristics, and learning profile with the selected intervention is most critical.

BROAD APPROACHES VERSUS STRATEGIES FOR INTERVENTION

It is important to understand what constitutes a broad-based, theoretically grounded, evidence-based approach as well as what constitutes an empirically validated strategy. In the context of this book, an approach is an intervention meant to address multiple aspects of the child's functioning, including core impairments and associated challenges, a wraparound approach in many ways. For example, applied behavioral analysis (ABA) can be considered a broad-based approach when applied in a comprehensive program to teach skills, modify behavior, and address behavioral problems large and small. Strategies such as direct teaching, reinforcement, prompting, chaining of behaviors, and promoting generalization are grounded in behavioral analysis, but each alone does not constitute a comprehensive ABA approach to intervention. Nevertheless, these strategies can be utilized independently and effectively, as long as the principles that underlie the strategy are properly understood. It is helpful to know how particular interventions have been tested, in order to understand under what conditions they have demonstrated efficacy. In this way, strategies can be applied and modified to fit the situation. Consequently, when an intervention does not give the desired result, we can step back from the strategy and consider the broader context to solve the problem.

Consider Casey, a 4-year old girl diagnosed with autism. Casey's social and adaptive skills are at the 1- to 2-year level; her cognitive profile reveals moderate delays in problem-solving ability; and her language profile shows receptive language at a 3-year level, with expressive skills at the 2.5-year level. Casey ignores other people—in fact she actively avoids them—and spends her time in self-stimulatory activity, swinging strings or other flexible items and watching them closely. She responds with single words when prompted but makes no social or even practical initiations toward others (even to request the bathroom).

In Casey's situation, promoting social development is important, but it must be done within a comprehensive treatment program in which foundational skills such as imitation, joint attention skills, following an adult's lead, and tolerating interaction with adults and peers are taught. The severity of Casey's autism, her active avoidance of interaction, and her preoccupation with self-stimulatory activity may require a wraparound program, that is, a broad-based approach in which all areas of weakness are dealt with comprehensively and in a highly structured, unified way. The two approaches profiled at the end of this chapter are examples of the very kind of broad-based approach that Casey might need.

In contrast, a child with mild ASD, with above-average cognitive functioning and low-average language skills, but with clear social impairments, may do well in an environment with typical children of his age, as long as he is taught some specific social behaviors, using strategies that fit the problem, the context, and the resources available. The program must be crafted to meet the individual needs of the child.

BEHAVIORAL AND DEVELOPMENTAL APPROACHES TO SOCIAL COMPETENCY

The field of ASD intervention has swung between the extremes of a strict behavioral approach to a fully developmental approach. Behavioral approaches are based on an understanding of how environmental responses modify an individual's behavior, by shaping or perhaps increasing the frequency and intensity of behavior, or by decreasing or extinguishing the behavior. Developmental approaches are those that consider the child's physical, emotional, social, and behavior development over time as critical to understanding how and what a child is ready to learn. Discrete skills and abilities are taught in developmental sequence and pitched to the child's level of comprehension and natural interest. At this juncture, it seems clear that neither approach, applied dogmatically, can address all the learning needs of children with ASD, particularly social learning needs (Prizant & Wetherby, 1998). Current approaches based on a comprehensive theoretical framework incorporate behavioral and developmental concepts and strategies in a sophisticated way (Odom, Boyd, Hall, & Hume, 2010; Vismara & Rogers, 2010). They address core impairments and associated symptoms in children and teens with ASD.

Chapter 5 covers evidence-based strategies for working with children on social goals. Here, two broad-based approaches for promoting social and overall competency in individuals with ASD are presented as examples: the Early Start Denver Model (Rogers & Dawson, 2010) and Pivotal Response Treatments (Koegel & Kern Koegel, 2006).

The Early Start Denver Model for Young Children With Autism

The Early Start Denver Model is an approach to working with very young children with autism that considers the biological and developmental processes of social, emotional, and communicative growth in young children, and how these processes can be engaged and enhanced in children with ASD through focused intervention (Rogers & Dawson, 2010). This approach successfully integrates a naturalistic behavioral approach within the context of a sophisticated understanding of child development. The curriculum focuses on receptive and expressive communication, joint attention, imitation, social skills, play skills, cognitive skills, fine and gross motor skills, and self-care skills. These are taught by professionals from different disciplines, such as occupational therapy and speech-language pathology, in an integrated way. In this sense, although specialists help to design the intervention for a child depending on their expertise, all professionals involved with the child implement the interventions. The learning activities are part of play and use strategies from ABA in formal and naturalistic teaching paradigms. For example, children may be taught basic skills, such as attending to the adult, following the adult's lead, and imitating, as well as more complex behavioral sequences. Critical teaching practices include the following:

- Adults modulate and optimize child affect, arousal, and attentional state.

- Adults display clear positive affect throughout teaching activities.
- Turn-taking and dyadic engagement occur throughout interactions.
- Adults respond to the child's communicative cues with sensitivity.
- Multiple, varied opportunities occur for social communication between children and adults, including opportunities to request, protest, comment, ask for help, greet, name, and so on.
- The therapist helps the child expand and elaborate on play activities.
- Adult language is pitched to the child's level of understanding.
- Transitions are managed effectively.

Language use by adults is characterized by the "one-up" rule, in which the average length of the adults' comments and responses to children is approximately one word longer than the child's average comments and responses. Further emphasized in this treatment model is the need to work with children to promote heightened, positive affect during interaction as a way to promote the child's interest and motivation to engage in and continue with social interaction. Another important component is family involvement, that is, coaching parents in the strategies utilized by therapists in the Early Start Denver Model so that they can carry on these activities throughout their child's day as opportunities arise. The model incorporates explicit goals for parents as part of the program. Helping parents learn to be advocates for their child is emphasized. Further, the model provides information about how to develop objectives, devise teaching plans, teach specific skills, and evaluate progress. This comprehensive approach has a strong evidence base to support its efficacy.

Pivotal Response Treatments for Autism

Pivotal Response Treatments (PRT) is a model for intervention that aims to help children with ASD learn and grow in an inclusive setting so they may take advantage of the learning and leisure opportunities offered to their typically developing peers. The essential idea behind this approach is that if children can master certain core skills of social development, these skills will result in changes in behavior across settings and people. So, pivotal responses are behaviors that, when mastered, will have a broad impact on the child's behavior. For example, children with ASD have trouble with self-initiation, meaning that they do not routinely initiate interactions to ask for help, to ask to play, to make a comment, or to clarify a request or instruction. Targeting self-initiation as a pivotal behavior and teaching self-initiation using PRT strategies will help the child initiate consistently in multiple settings and with different people. This newly learned behavior helps the child to be more interactive and more involved in all activities throughout the day.

PRT is a developmental approach to intervention that makes use of the principles of ABA (Koegel & Koegel, 1995; Koegel, Koegel, & Camerata, 2010). Intervention is designed based on the child's current developmental level and the behaviors the child is expected to perform in various settings. Taking this information as a starting point, the interventionist arranges the environment and the interactions with the child to create frequent opportunities to implement the stimulus-response-reinforcement teaching sequence that is the root of ABA. In this regard, the learning opportunity is embedded in the day-to-day life of the child as opposed to being imposed in an artificial learning environment. For example, if the objective is to teach a child to request, a more traditional ABA approach using the discrete trial technique would involve having the child practice making requests following a cue (stimulus) from the interventionist, and then receiving a reinforcement such as an edible treat or a sticker after successfully completing multiple trials of the sequence. The child may master requesting in this situation, but whether he will make requests in his usual environment throughout his day is uncertain. A PRT approach would be to set up the environment so that the child can see a desired item (e.g., toy, edible) out of reach, and then teach the child to request in order to receive the item. Once he makes the request, he is given the item (allowed to play with the toy or eat the treat). In this case, PRT makes use of the natural environment and the child's particular desires as the designated stimulus and reinforcer. The likelihood that the child will learn the sequence of requesting and will use this new skill in multiple settings is increased, since he has learned that his behavior has agency that can result in changes in others' behavior. That is, he can get what he desires by requesting.

The PRT model does not include a specialized curriculum for children with ASD; it is meant to be implemented using the general education curriculum as a guide for both academic and social learning. The emphasis is on the method of teaching versus the content of the lessons. PRT makes use of natural environments for teaching and learning, since this is where the child must apply newly learned knowledge and behaviors. Using the child's preferences to guide learning opportunities, the interventionist manipulates the environment to promote new learning. Any attempt on the child's part to respond appropriately is reinforced, so that the child will stay motivated to engage with others. Further, toys and activities that are motivating to all children in the particular setting are included in order to incorporate typically developing peers into play and social interaction with the child with ASD. The adult facilitates social interaction by supporting the children's commenting, requesting, and helping one another. The child with ASD learns that interaction facilitates fun and increased opportunities for learning new games and activities. If the child will be engaged in a new activity, the interventionist may use priming, a technique of reviewing the activity and perhaps practicing some aspects of it prior to the actual experience.

An important component of PRT is that parents are taught how to implement the intervention strategies so they can create learning opportunities throughout the child's day. Further, as parents implement PRT in the home, the child and the parent learn from each other; the parent learns what kinds of activities and items are reinforcing, and has the opportunity to test out novel activities and toys to see what piques the child's interest. Parents and other interventionists communicate regularly about this issue and the child's progress, so that all are working together to enlarge the child's world and draw her closer to activities appropriate to her developmental age. In this way, nonfunctional play and repetitive activities can be replaced by functional play routines and other adaptive activities.

Children whose parents have been trained in PRT are more likely to make gains than children whose parents have not been trained. Further, paraprofessionals who are trained, for example, to facilitate social interaction using the PRT approach are more likely to implement intervention effectively compared with those who have not been trained. Thus far, the model has identified five behaviors as pivotal for having a broad-based impact on children's learning: motivation, self-initiation, responsivity to multiple cues, self-management, and empathy. Many children with ASD show minimal motivation to interact with others or participate in age-appropriate activities. Targeting motivation addresses this problem and increases the likelihood that the child will be engaged in the wider world more consistently. Koegel, Koegel, Vernon, and Brookman-Frazee (2010) speculated that the child with ASD may begin with some motivation to engage others, but since he does not have the tools and skills to do so, initiations are not met with encouragement and engagement. Thus over time the child becomes less motivated to interact. "Pivotal Response Treatment (PRT) focuses on decreasing the presence of learned helplessness by enhancing the relationship between the children's responses and their contingent acquisition of reinforcers" (p. 328). PRT includes techniques to promote motivation, for example, child choice of activities, variation of tasks (so the child stays interested), and the use of natural reinforcers.

Teaching self-initiation, another pivotal behavior, promotes self-advocacy and engagement with others. It may reduce disruptive behaviors since the child learns to ask for what he needs rather than becoming upset because he has no way to communicate his requests or wants to others. Further, the degree to which children can self-initiate predicts long-term outcome (Koegel, Koegel, Vernon, et al., 2010).

Children with ASD may show stimulus overselectivity, that is, an intense focus on an irrelevant detail of an object or activity (stimulus) that impedes learning the correct response. For example, a child might become absorbed with clocks and wristwatches in every environment, to the exclusion of other environmental cues. To address stimulus overselectivity, the pivotal behavior of responsivity to multiple cues is taught. The child learns to observe and integrate multiple cues when confronted with a particular situation. Paying attention to multiple elements reduces the possibility that the child will perseverate on irrelevant information.

Self-management allows the child to take greater responsibility for executing newly learned behavior. A child might be taught to use a wrist counter, checklist, a palm pilot, or a cell phone to keep track of how frequently she asks a question in class, if this is a targeted skill for self-management. Frequency is one measure that may be used, but other more complex measures can be used for more complex skills. A visual schedule can be placed on a cell phone using the iPrompt application so that an older child can remember a sequence of steps needed to wrap up the school day, select materials he needs for homework, and get to the bus on time. Teaching self-management reduces reliance on external prompts from adults.

Finally, empathy is a pivotal behavior that, when taught, will increase the chances that the child engages with peers and is accepted by them. Children are taught explicitly to recognize common situations in which other people might need an empathic response and then are taught ways to understand and respond verbally to the situation. Koegel and Koegel (2006) suggested that some children with ASD are capable of feeling empathy yet do not have the skills to recognize situations that are distressing to others unless they are explicitly described. Further, the children need instruction on how to express their concern for others appropriately.

These two comprehensive models, the Early Start Denver Model and Pivotal Response Treatments, incorporate many of the strategies for teaching described in Chapter 5. What is striking about these and other comprehensive models is that they emphasize the need to understand the child in a developmental context, and the intervention addresses all areas of impairment in ASD. Too often we consider social functioning to refer only to an individual's ability to have social relationships for recreational purposes and purposes of personal satisfaction. While this is true, social functioning encompasses almost everything we do throughout the day and is absolutely necessary for full participation, independent living, and economic self-sufficiency.

CHAPTER THREE

Integration: The Key to Effective Intervention

• •

The best-laid plans for intervention can go awry if key components are not well integrated. What this means is that the team
must be working as a fully functioning unit, with shared understanding of the child, the social goals, and the means for
accomplishing these goals. In this way, the child gains greater
understanding of ongoing social interaction as well as how social interaction and friendships work in general. In some ways,
an integrated approach to intervention is even more important
when teaching social competency skills and behaviors than for
teaching other skills. Think about it in this way: Children with
ASD struggle with a world that can appear fragmented, so that
visual and auditory cues, or verbal and nonverbal contextual
cues, do not come together for them when trying to learn a
skill or solve a problem. Many children focus on details without grasping the whole. This bias results in reduced understanding of the problem and the world. Since social information is complex and varies with time and place, social problem
solving is even more difficult than solving other kinds of problems. For example, a seventh grade student in a self-contained
classroom in a public school setting must learn what behaviors are acceptable in the classroom and what behaviors are
acceptable in the larger school environment, since these may

differ. If we are to help children develop social competency, we must help them make links between pieces of social information in their world, so they can draw broader conclusions than they might if left on their own.

It turns out that providing integrated treatment is more complex than it sounds. First, we must understand the following:

1. The child's learning profile, which includes information about the child's current level of social and adaptive functioning as well as the cognitive and language profile (as determined by formal testing)
2. The family issues
3. The relevant learning goals for the child
4. The plan for teaching and generalizing skills
5. The methods for measuring progress.

Second, we need an explicit plan for establishing collaborative relationships and engaging in ongoing communication with all members of the child's team. In this context, the team includes the parents of the child, the regular education teacher (if involved), the special education teacher, a school administrator, and other specialists such as the speech-language pathologist or occupational therapist, as well as the pediatrician, mental health counselors, family counselors, and other community providers.

As an example, consider a third grade student with autism, who, despite above-average intellectual abilities, cannot tolerate waiting for a turn or not being first for every activity that occurs at school. The child's reaction when he has to wait or not be first to do something varies from irritation and complaining to a full-blown tantrum. The child's peers avoid him because of what they perceive as his self-centered, babyish behavior. While he would like to develop friendships, the child

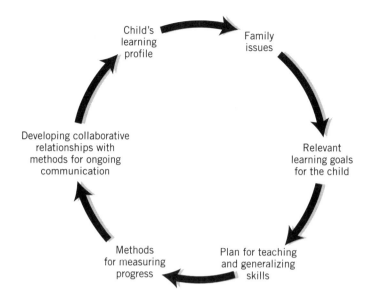

Figure 3-1. Key ingredients for effective intervention.

makes no connection between his difficult behavior and his social isolation. The classroom teacher and occupational therapist work with the child regularly, stressing the need to cooperate with peers and adults to gain social acceptance, but this
is only partially effective. They teach strategies for waiting and
tolerating frustration, which are partially effective, but the
child does not apply these in diverse contexts throughout the
school day. What is needed is extensive, strategic practice in
every setting the child is exposed to, throughout the day, every
day! Every adult who interacts with the child—the parents,
gym teacher, playground monitor, music teacher, speech pathologist, school librarian, school psychologist, assistant prin-
cipal, and resource room teacher—needs to be cognizant of
the child's difficulty and actively help him practice more adaptive skills. These adults supplement the core team planning for
the child's intervention (see Chapter 6). It may be appropriate

for adults to involve other children in the practice experience, since this may be more reinforcing for the child. In a school setting, one might need to obtain permission from the parents of the affected child to involve peers, but since peers will be quite aware of the child's struggles, it may not be difficult to convince parents to allow this to happen, in the service of improving the child's social skills and increasing social acceptance.

This chapter describes the components of an integrated intervention approach in brief, with greater elaboration in subsequent chapters. The take-home message here is that without a synergistic approach to intervention, gains are likely to be spotty and not necessarily sustained.

UNDERSTANDING THE CHILD'S LEARNING PROFILE AND CURRENT FUNCTIONING

Before any plan is made to address social learning for a child with an ASD, the treatment team must have a well-rounded picture of the child's level of social and adaptive functioning as well as comprehensive knowledge of the child's learning profile. The best way to develop this understanding is to combine information from standard assessment instruments with the observations and impressions of parents and professionals. This includes assessments of functioning with respect to day-to-day activities, social behavior, and maladaptive behavior. This gives the team a starting point for identifying goals and developing behavioral objectives. A firm understanding of these issues up front goes a long way when devising strategies for teaching social behavior.

Two excellent measures of adaptive and social functioning in children with ASD are the Vineland Adaptive Behavior Scales (VABS), second edition (Sparrow, Cicchetti, & Balla, 2005), and the Pervasive Developmental Disorders Behavioral Inventory (PPD-BI; Cohen & Sudhalter, 2005). Each has the advantage of providing parent and teacher forms so that multiple perspectives can be gathered and integrated. You should not necessarily expect consistency between results from teachers and parents since all children behave differently in different settings and with different people. It is not likely to be the case that the results of one assessment are more valid than the results of another; in fact, evaluations of children using measures of behavior more often than not show minimal agreement (De Los Reyes & Kazdin, 2005). So this inconsistency is to be expected, and we can mine these discrepancies for clues to how and why the child performs well in one setting or with a particular task, but not so well in a different setting or when completing a different task. This information is key for understanding why some skills and behaviors have generalized across settings and others have not.

The VABS is a valid and reliable measure of adaptive functioning, appropriate for individuals from ages 2 to 90 years (Sparrow et al., 2005). The VABS provides an assessment of an individual's functioning compared to same-age peers with regard to communication, daily living, socialization, and motor skills. In each of these domains, the VABS provides a standard score that reflects the individual's level of functioning as compared with typically developing, same-age peers. Further, each domain contains three subdomains, which give detailed information about areas of competency and difficulty. For example, the socialization domain includes three subdomains: interpersonal relationships, play and leisure skills, and coping skills. These subdomain assessments give nuanced information about strengths and weaknesses in socialization, and this information provides the basis for choosing goals and developing behavioral objectives. Further, the VABS measures maladaptive behavior, which is important for gauging how or why an individual with age-appropriate positive behaviors might have trouble functioning in daily life.

The VABS can be administered as a parent interview, a parent rating form, or a teacher rating form (Sparrow, Cicchetti, & Balla, 2006). These forms are equally valid and reliable. The parent interview form can be particularly useful because the interviewer develops a rapport with parents that helps to facilitate a therapeutic relationship. Further, in detailed discussion about day-to-day life, parents may develop a new perspective on their child and her developmental challenges. Some parents have limited knowledge about how typical development progresses, such that they may not appreciate the degree of their child's impairment. Others may expect more from their child than is reasonable, again leading to a mismatch between parent demands and the child's performance. Finally, some parents become so accustomed to behavioral difficulties, such as aggression, that they cease to see it as aberrant and in need of intervention. A mother may report that her 6-year-old son behaves fairly well, but then disclose that the child has tantrums about five times daily for 20 minutes at a time. She implements various strategies each day to keep him under control, as well as avoiding public places. In this situation, this mother has become so accustomed to her son's behavior that she does not consider it to be outside the norm.

An additional advantage of the VABS is that it has been designed with particular attention to the assessment of typical behavior associated with social development (Sparrow et al., 2005). The second edition includes normative information based on a population of individuals with ASDs. In the context of planning an intervention for a child with ASD, the VABS can help the user to consider how the child compares to other children with a similar disability with regard to a particular domain of functioning.

The PDD-BI is a valid and reliable instrument that provides standard scores for individual domains of functioning as well as composite scores (Cohen, Schmidt-Lackner, Romanczyk, & Sudhalter, 2003). This instrument focuses on the core deficits of ASDs as well as the associated challenges (e.g., aggression), and further, the instrument is designed to assess behavioral change in response to intervention. This is one of the first instruments available that combines a nuanced approach to the assessment of the social-communication impairment in pervasive developmental disorders along with rigorous psychometrics. Individual domains of assessment include sensory and perceptual approach behaviors; rituals and resistance to change behavior; social pragmatic problems; semantic and pragmatic problems; arousal regulation problems; specific fears; aggressiveness; social approach behaviors; expressive language; and learning, memory, and receptive language. The PDD-BI domains are used to calculate composite scores and an autism composite score.

In summary, the PDD-BI and the VABS, second edition, provide comprehensive information about a child's usual behavior, making it possible for the team to construct a picture of the child's day-to-day functioning. For example, the team can clarify the following:

- Is the child able to perform self-care skills, such as dressing, toileting, and eating in public at the same level as same-age peers?
- Does the child have behavioral problems (outbursts) or unusual behaviors that set him or her apart from peers?
- Is the child interested in interacting with peers?
- Does the child approach or ignore other children?

- Are play initiation behaviors appropriate?
- Does the child know how to respond to an invitation to play?
- Does the child know how to play games and engage in activities that peers are doing?
- Does the child know how to take turns, follow rules, and share materials?
- Does the child pick up on nonverbal cues and understand nonliteral language?

Once the team has a comprehensive picture of the child's adaptive and social functioning, the next step is to obtain information about the child's learning profile, which includes the cognitive and language profile. With regard to the cognitive profile, the psychologist on the team selects the most appropriate measure of developmental level, IQ or conceptual ability from a number of available standardized instruments. The particular measures are chosen based on which measures will provide the most detailed information about the child. Thus, the psychologist who conducts the cognitive assessment is well positioned to help the educational team understand how peaks and valleys in the child's cognitive profile will influence the child's ability to learn. A child may do well with reasoning tasks when provided with visual supports, but do more poorly when asked to reason based on heard information only. Another child may show strong rote memory skills for learning new information but be less able to use flexible strategies for manipulating information to draw novel conclusions.

Children with ASD may have impairments in executive functioning skills, including the ability to organize information, to plan activities or learn systematically, to revise learning strategies that are not working, or to delay impulsive responding when presented with problem situations (Tsatsanis, 2005). Armed with this information, the educational team can examine the chosen intervention strategies for meeting a particular objective in the light of the child's unique cognitive profile.

As well as strengths and weaknesses in the cognitive profile, a child with an ASD will show strengths and weaknesses with regard to language and communication (Klin, Saulnier, Tsatsanis, & Volkmar, 2005). Once again, the speech-language pathologist on the team selects the appropriate standardized tests from a host of available language measures, depending on the child's communication problems. The speech-language pathologist can interpret the results of the assessment so the team can understand how the child understands and uses language.

The question of language use is much more complicated than it seems. Children with ASDs have significant impairments in understanding and using language that may be far greater than parents or teachers appreciate (Tager-Flusberg, Paul, & Lord, 2005). It is not uncommon to hear parents say that their child "understands everything" but simply chooses not to comply with parental requests. In our clinical work at Yale, we often find that a child relies on the routine and predictability of the home situation to comply with parental requests, so that he can perform at home or in familiar situations although his actual understanding of language is far more limited. Parents and teachers may be fooled into believing that the child is more capable than he really is because much of what is required of him happens in a familiar context. The child responds based on past experience rather than processing new information. The formal speech and language assessment determines the child's level of language understanding and usage, and this assessment must go beyond testing expressive or receptive vocabulary. The speech-language pathologist can provide the team with information regarding the child's receptive and expressive language, correct use of grammar and syntax, comprehension, and understanding of the pragmatics of communication, which include the ability to know how to take turns in conversation, stay on topic, and interpret nonverbal cues that give information about the speaker and the topic, as well as other nuances necessary for smooth reciprocal conversation. This information guides choices about how to teach new information to the child, as well as the appropriate targets for language learning.

Also important for social language learning is the ability of individuals to construct a narrative, that is, to be able to tell a story about something they have done, something they saw, or something they intend to do (Loth, 2008). As described in detail in Chapter 1, the ability to use language to sequence information, for example, "First I did this, then I did that," helps an individual create a template for recording and understanding experiences. When children have this ability, it helps them predict what might happen in their lives and gives them a sense of themselves and what the world is about. Children and teenagers on the autism spectrum have trouble with this kind of abstract construction of a narrative (Loth, 2008). This makes their world confusing and unpredictable. Hence, there is a need to use formal assessment and informal methods to gauge a child's ability to narrate experiences.

RELEVANT FAMILY ISSUES

So often there is conflict within families or between families and professionals regarding how to understand the child, what the child's needs are, the best methods for intervening, and the most accurate and valid ways to measure progress. The source of the conflict may be genuine disagreement about how well the child is doing or what the child is capable of doing or learning. More often than not, these disagreements are played out in the context of mistrust among family and team members, or between professionals from different disciplines or between family and nonfamily members. All members of the team deal with pressure from the community at large about how they should parent, teach, or intervene, and all cope with expectations about how the child should progress. These factors influence how well the team functions and ultimately how well the child will do with regard to developing social competency. The issues are discussed in greater detail in Chapter 6, but it is important to highlight them, since underlying issues can surface unexpectedly when planning a child's program.

THE GOALS FOR SOCIAL LEARNING

To identify the social learning goals that are most appropriate for the child, the team must define what behaviors the child needs to learn or improve to move toward age-appropriate levels. This process has to be based on a solid understanding of how typical children develop (as described in Chapter 1), so that goals and objectives can be appropriate based on the child's current level of development and the expectations of the peer group. Without a comprehensive understanding of the foundational skills that underlie more complex social behavior (see Figure 1-1), new social behaviors are not likely to be well integrated into a child's social repertoire. These behaviors may look artificial and lead to alienation rather than acceptance from peers. Figure 3-2 includes a list of some of the skills we try to teach when working with children with ASD.

Further, if the child engages in atypical, negative, and possibly destructive behavior, these behaviors must be targeted along with goals for developing positive social behavior. Children with atypical or difficult behaviors can develop a negative reputation among their peers that is extraordinarily difficult to counteract. The more quickly and completely these behaviors can be addressed, the greater chance the child has in making social inroads with peers. Atypical behaviors might include

- Looks at communicative partner
- Responds to his or her name
- Seeks contact with others
- Imitates others
- Recognizes faces and facial expressions
- Shares emotional states with others
- Interprets tone of voice
- Uses nonverbal communication strategies
- Indicates preferences
- Responds to bids for joint attention
- Initiates joint attention
- Uses word approximations
- Plays with cause-and-effect toys
- Plays in parallel with others/plays make-believe
- Greets others
- Follows rules/takes turns in play/develops logical sequences for play
- Develops self-advocacy skills appropriate to age
- Engages in symbolic use of toys/pretend play with others
- Develops narrative skills
- Understands personal boundaries
- Initiates social contact
- Offers to help others without prompting
- Learns not to make inappropriate comments
- Develops elaborate pretend play/practicing of roles
- Converses with adults and peers on topics of interest to others
- Negotiates simple conflicts successfully
- Accepts the need to relax interpretation of rules based on context
- Understands rules for privacy for self and others
- Develops understanding of own emotions/regulates behavior
- Understands age/gender-appropriate behavior/Negotiates relationships successfully
- Understands figures of speech, idioms
- Takes care of appearance independently
- Copes with teasing
- Develops self-monitoring skills
- Shows appropriate modesty related to strengths
- Copes with rejection
- Apologizes when indicated
- Makes reasonable judgments about people and activities
- Expresses affection appropriately
- Manages conflict with adults appropriately
- Manages time and work responsibilities

Figure 3-2. Skills frequently targeted for intervention.

motor mannerisms or complex stereotypic behavior, such as rocking, pacing, twirling, or unusual body posturing. Another manifestation of repetitive behavior might be repetitive questioning or commenting to adults or peers, which annoys others. These behaviors may occur when the child feels stressed or simply at loose ends. While not harmful in and of themselves for the most part, these behaviors can stigmatize a child, causing peers to avoid interaction.

Let's take some examples. Chloé is a fifth grader who tends to make repeated comments to other girls in her class, complimenting their clothing or their humorous behavior. While offering a compliment is a positive social behavior, Chloé does this so frequently that it appears artificial and robotic. Initially her classmates responded positively, but of late they either ignore her comments or offer mocking replies in return. If ignored, Chloé steps up the frequency of her comments, eliciting even greater irritation from her peers. If a response is sarcastic, Chloé fails to recognize this and tends to pursue the interaction, which sets her up for ongoing teasing from her peers. While Chloé has been taught some positive social behaviors, she is not able to differentiate when the behavior is appropriate and when it becomes excessive and annoying. Without further intervention, she will likely continue to have trouble developing peer relationships.

In this situation, the educational team might devise a plan to help Chloé keep count of how often she makes a comment or asks a question, and set parameters with her about when she must stop. They might help her identify ways to discern whether she is annoying other kids, or teach her strategies to recognize and then respond to comments that are critical. This will require extensive teaching, but it is as important to Chloé's social acceptance and ongoing social functioning as is learning new, positive social behaviors.

As a second example, a school team may notice that Ben, a

child with an ASD, laughs when he sees that another child has hurt himself or is crying. The other children note Ben's non-empathic responses and remark on them. The children regard Ben as uncaring, and they begin to isolate him. Adults explain this behavior by commenting that Ben "has autism." When they see Ben laughing, they correct him by saying, "That's inappropriate." Some teachers will even tell other students that Ben does not understand the particular situation well. These efforts are well and good but do not go far enough.

Ben has limited ability to empathize with others nor does he read and interpret facial expressions at the same skill level as peers. Further, given his poor perspective-taking skills, he cannot appreciate the level of distress another child feels and he has no idea that his behavior is viewed negatively. At the same time, Ben actually likes other kids and wants to have friends.

In such a situation, a more intensive intervention is necessary. Ben's team must consider what gaps in basic social understanding and behavior underlie Ben's socially inappropriate behavior (Figure 3-3). Simply extinguishing the inappropriate behavior without helping Ben behave more adaptively has very limited value. As a beginning, Ben might work one on one with an adult, using photographs or images to learn to recognize different facial expressions. To promote generalization of his understanding, these images would include babies, young children, older children, teens and adults, and people of different races. He may work with an adult to recognize facial expressions in peers around the school environment. Ben can be taught explicitly how facial expressions provide clues to how others are feeling and what behavioral responses are appropriate. Part of the intervention might be learning about common situations that happen among peers or between students and teachers, with explicit instruction about why people behave the way they do. Helping Ben look for multiple cues in

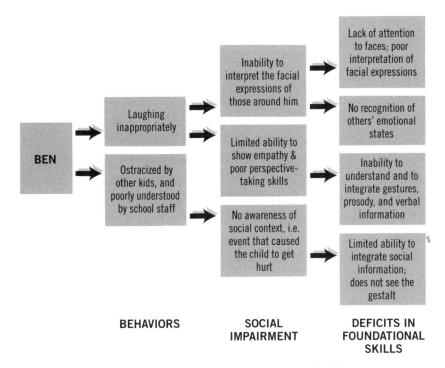

Figure 3-3. The sources and consequences of Ben's behavior.

his environment as a way to make accurate interpretations of the social context is important. What are the other kids doing? Throughout this intervention, Ben will need reinforcement for learning, and the intervention team will need to set up situations to help Ben practice and promote skill development throughout the school year. Parents should be involved as well, supporting Ben's learning in this situation.

To begin the process of selecting developmentally appropriate goals, the team must identify gaps in the child's social and emotional behavior, as well as identifying the foundational skills that support that particular skill in a typically developing child (Figure 1-1). Foundational skills such as sensory learning, emotional regulation, and receptive and expressive language understanding support the development of more complex skills.

A PLAN FOR TEACHING AND GENERALIZING SKILLS

Once the intervention team has selected goals for social learning for a particular child, behavioral objectives must be devised and strategies for teaching developed. Within the school context, this blueprint of goals for a child is known as the individual education plan (IEP). Figure 3-4 shows a sample of a section where goals and objectives are listed.

The challenge is translating these goals into skills and behaviors to be learned, and selecting the intervention strategy that best matches the child. Chapter 4 describes this process and Chapter 5 includes extensive information regarding evidence-based strategies and best practices available to help children learn new skills and promote their social development. All will not work equally well with all children; the current intervention literature gives us limited information on what works for whom. Interventionists must use their best judgment based on their knowledge of the child, and perhaps what strategies have worked in the past, as well as their knowledge of ASD, to design or select an appropriate intervention.

Let's compare two scenarios. A school team is concerned about John's isolation on the playground during recess. John is 10 years old and spends most of his time in a resource room for academic work. He is mildly intellectually disabled and his receptive and language skills are lower than what would be expected given his intellectual disability. John is mainstreamed for art, music, gym, computers, and recess and a paraprofessional is with him at those times to help him participate appropriately in those experiences. At recess he tends to walk the perimeter of the schoolyard unless his paraprofessional arranges for him to participate in a game such as tag. John will

| Student | Frank C | | DOB | 8/19/2004 |
| District | Suffolk | Date | 5/10/2010 | |

Measurable Annual Goal	*Frank will engage with peers during recess*	Evaluation Procedure	Dates of Evaluation
Objective 1	Frank will initiate a conversation with a peer three times out of five recess opportunities per week.	Frank self-reports to teacher each day. Playground monitor documents initiation and notes to whom Frank speaks and for how long; reports to teacher daily.	6/10/10 6/30/10 9/10/10 etc.
Objective 2	Frank will join the play with at least one other child; once per week.	Direct observation by special education teacher.	6/10/10 etc.
Objective 3	Frank will use appropriate language during interactions with peers.	Direct observation of special education teacher, playground monitor will tally any instances of inappropriate language. Frank will self-monitor and report to special education teacher.	6/10/10 etc.

Figure 3-4. Example of an IEP page listing goals and objectives.

do this, and the other children tolerate it, but it does not lead to any meaningful or sustained interaction with other children.

A goal for social development on John's IEP is that he "enter into and sustain play with his peers for 10 minutes during each recess period." The school social worker selects a social story about joining other children in play, and she reads this to John during her one-to-one session with him for several days in a row. In the story, a boy approaches peers and asks if he can play ("Can I play with you?"). The peers welcome him, and he joins in. The social worker asks John if he thinks he can do this. He says that he can, and he tests it out.

The social worker watches as John attempts to implement his newly learned strategy. Out on the playground, he approaches an exuberant girl organizing a game of tag, but he cannot seem to get her attention. The game gets started, and he tries to get involved, but the other children do not know that he is playing, and they ignore him. John runs around for the duration of the recess period but is not really part of the game. He seems somewhat pleased and somewhat confused, not really knowing if he is involved or not. The recess period comes to an end.

John's team is discouraged by his lack of success but quickly understands that, given his vulnerabilities in verbal skills, he was not able to communicate quickly with the leader of the playground game, and he needs another strategy to help him get involved. The team just isn't sure what to do. In this example, John's team has banked on the fact that he knows how to play tag as he has played before with support from a paraprofessional. Despite his strong social interest, John is in no way as verbally adept as he needs to be to find a place in this game.

An alternative strategy might be to pair John up with a peer tutor, a child who has agreed to help John be a part of the games at recess. This tutor has had some specific coaching in this role (see Chapter 5) and understands that she can facilitate John's participation in the game. The tutor provides explicit directions to John and the other players about his participation in the game and supports the other children as they take steps to include him. Other children follow the lead of the tutor and begin to involve John in this game and other games on the playground. The norm for recess in this classroom becomes one in which children incorporate John into the play, with the understanding that he has trouble doing it on his own.

In this situation, the use of a social story was worth a try, but the heavy reliance on understanding language and then holding the information about the play entry strategy in mind while applying it in a fast-moving environment was too much for John. Given his cognitive and communication limitations, John was not going to be able to negotiate entry into this social situation independently. He clearly needed ongoing adult and peer support.

In a second scenario, a boy named Nick, with above-average cognitive skills and average formal language skills is isolated on the playground during recess. Nick tends to walk around the perimeter of the schoolyard while other children engage in various games. At times, Nick approaches other children and attempts conversation, but his topics are so unusual in content—electromagnetic transducers and actuators—that other kids tend to shy away. The educational team would like to see Nick more involved but do not know how to make this happen.

Nick's team considers engaging one or two peer tutors to help Nick integrate into the play during recess. They select two boys whom they think will be willing and able and provide some specific coaching about how to include Nick in the games during recess. Nick is agreeable to staying close to the mentors during recess, and the special education teacher instructs Nick not to discuss electromagnetics with the other boys. After some argument with his teacher, Nick agrees to this rule.

Nick and his mentors play together during recess, and Nick is able to play tag and other active games with the other kids. So far, the intervention seems to be a success. Nick's team notices, however, that the other children allow Nick to play but do not engage in conversation with him when the game is over (when lining up to go inside or finding a seat for lunch). Nick's mentors seem a bit tired of him as well, dropping their interaction as soon as a game ends on the playground. Nick makes remarks to the other kids about videos or television shows, but his comments seem a bit out of the blue, and he tends to say the same thing again and again. Nick notices that the kids seem to be ignoring him, so he steps up the frequency of his comments, and finally lapses into a monologue about fluorescent lamps as transducers. While most kids keep their distance, some start to mock him. The mentors avoid Nick entirely at this point.

In this situation, giving Nick explicit instructions about not talking about his special interest in electromagnetics makes sense, but Nick needs instructions about what to talk about and how. Practice with an adult in a one-on-one situation, choosing topics of interest to Nick and to other kids his age is warranted. This instruction should begin with simple rules about topics, turn-taking in conversation, and progress to asking questions, responding to comments, and elaborating on topics. Learning when to be quiet might be important for these situations. To evaluate what can be expected of Nick in terms of making progress, the team will have to consider whether Nick can learn that conversation is not just information exchange but a way of developing an emotional connection to another person. This is a pretty abstract concept to teach and for a child with ASD to understand.

Another issue at play here is that Nick resorts to talking

about his unusual topics when he becomes anxious or does not know what to do. On the playground, when he becomes vaguely aware that his comments are not helping his interactions, he lapses into what are safe topics for him, without appreciating how odd they seem to his peers. Here, his challenges with perspective taking and understanding age-appropriate conversational topics get in his way. Intervention for this behavior must go beyond teaching Nick about how to maintain conversation on topics of common interest to his peers. He must learn to monitor his emotional state to recognize when he is becoming anxious. If Nick can develop self-awareness about his internal state, he may be able to use specific strategies to reduce his anxiety rather than the nonfunctional one (the electromagnetics monologue) he is using now (see Cognitive-Behavioral Treatment in Chapter 5). In this example, helping Nick to develop social skills on the playground goes beyond providing him with some basic rules for interactions and engaging mentors to help him join a game. One can see that the intervention is quite complex, and thoughtful planning and practice will be required to execute it.

EVALUATING PROGRESS AND IDENTIFYING NEW GOALS

The IEP requires that the team identify annual goals and document the child's progress with respect to these goals. The language in the Individuals With Disabilities Education Improvement Act (2004) no longer requires specific behavioral objectives or benchmarks for progress (Wright & Wright, 2004). Further, progress does not necessarily have to be quantified, but it does need to be measurable, with the method of measurement stated up front. This is an interesting development for measuring progress on social goals for children with ASD. In some ways, it is a double-edged sword. Should an annual goal be written, "Helen will engage in reciprocal conversation with peers, three times weekly during recess," or should it read, "Helen will develop a mutual friendship with a peer in the fifth grade at Roosevelt Elementary School?" On one hand, using quantifiable terms such as frequency, duration, and rate provides objective information about the child's behavior. On the other hand, reciprocal conversation with peers three times weekly during recess does not necessarily constitute conversations between friends! The state of the science with regard to promoting social development in children and teens with ASD does not provide us with subtle, sophisticated measures of the quality of social relationships and interactions, at least not those that can be implemented in a school situation in short-term intervals. At the very least, creating observable, behavioral objectives for goals provides a framework for the team when designing interventions.

Many times, one sees an objective written with a benchmark for the frequency of behavior, for example, "Jack will respond to a comment by a peer 80% of the time." Measuring frequency is relevant, although practically, keeping an accurate measurement of Jack's responses might not be easy. Eighty percent of the time can be ascertained only by monitoring Jack 100% of the time. This is not particularly realistic for the intervention team. Moreover, this basic measurement scheme does not provide helpful information about why a behavior is or is not occurring. Has the instruction been clear and sufficient? Are the cues that help the child to carry out the behavior in place? Does the child have sufficient opportunities to carry out the behavior?

The team needs user-friendly and realistic ways of measuring behavior in the moment. This might be a simple checklist of a few behaviors, on which a teacher or paraprofessional documents an occurrence of a behavior. This would be shared by the team and tracked over time to assess the child's progress. Measurement is discussed in greater detail in Chapter 8.

Unfortunately, there is plenty of pressure to make things happen, but not a lot of explicit information about how to do it. The IEP cannot provide more than broad guidelines about how special education and related services will be utilized to help the child meet the annual goals. However, there is no reason why the team cannot develop a more explicit plan for teaching specific skills and behaviors, and reference this plan in the IEP.

At the same time, setting benchmarks for progress can create a huge amount of anxiety for the team, since, if the child fails to make progress, an initial assumption might be that the team has failed to do its job. Most educators take their work seriously and are invested in the child making progress. Believing that they are responsible for lack of progress is discouraging and frustrating. In fact, a child's lack of documented progress may be because the goals are too ambitious or broad, or the behavioral objectives do not include measurement of all the steps the child needs to master to meet a particular goal. In other situations, the strategy for teaching a new skill may be a good one but may not fit the child's learning style. Finally, a child may need more time or additional supports to master a particular new behavior.

Despite what we all might want, there are no clear-cut, unambiguous answers to how goals should be assigned, strategies selected, progress assessed, and revisions made. There are guidelines for working through these steps (described in Chapter 4) that need to be applied in an intelligent, reasonable, and sensible way, at the discretion of the child's intervention team.

ESTABLISHING COLLABORATIVE RELATIONSHIPS AND PLANNING FOR ONGOING COMMUNICATION WITHIN THE TEAM

While it sounds clichéd, it truly takes a village to develop and execute a plan to promote social development in a child with an ASD. Most of our days are filled with social interaction, whether we are socializing or not. Day-to-day functioning in school and community settings requires effective social interaction with a variety of people—whether a child is talking to a school crossing guard, the school librarian, the parent of a friend, the ballet teacher, or the baseball coach. For a child with an ASD, these encounters are just as complex as those that involve peers in a recreational setting. Thus, intervention to promote social development must target these interactions and experiences as well.

Obviously, there is no way to identify and anticipate each situation a child may encounter during a day or week, but the more that the child can learn appropriate and effective interaction skills in multiple environments, the better. The school setting is optimal for this, since the child will enter predictable environments, and all adults in the school setting are working to promote the child's education, growth, and development. A core of individuals within the school system are responsible for the child's education, including a representative of the administration, a regular education teacher, a special education teacher, parents, and possibly other professionals who provide related services in the school setting and also in the community. However, the core team should not hesitate to involve other teachers who interact with the student (in art, gym, study hall, music, or resource room) and the administrator should support this involvement. Since social interaction skills cut across every setting, it is untenable for any educator to decline involvement in the student's intervention.

When team members do not agree or there is animosity between school personnel, parents, or outside providers, it is the responsibility of the school district administrator participating in the team process to address the issue. A school team with internal divisions is not a functional team, and the impact of that dysfunction goes beyond the education of the particular child. Chapter 6 describes some of the common issues that arise as teams attempt to collaborate. One way to ensure ongoing communication is to make regular meetings of the team a requirement on the IEP, which allots time for comparing notes and brainstorming about the issues. It also helps with team morale since raising and educating a child with an ASD is a labor-intensive process. The emotional and psychological state of the family and of the professionals involved contributes to the smooth or not-so-smooth functioning of the group. Reminding the entire team of the long-term goals for the child and the likelihood that progress will proceed in fits and starts may help to keep the group grounded and realistic, with the ability to celebrate the child's small achievements as they lead toward broader goals.

CHAPTER FOUR

Designing Child-Specific Interventions

· ·

Chapters 1, 2, and 3 provide some examples of the kinds of social problems that children with ASD manifest and what learning challenges these problems present. Of course, in addition to learning a new social behavior, a child must learn to determine when and where a new behavior should be performed, how it might be modified to fit a particular context, and with whom the behavior is most appropriate, adults or peers. Social behavior is extraordinarily context specific and we must analyze a social context before acting. The details of the context provide the cues for what behavior is appropriate, but we must also grasp the whole picture.

We know there are evidence-based approaches (Chapter 2) and strategies (Chapter 5) for promoting social development and social skills in children with ASD, but how are therapists to know which approaches and strategies are most appropriate for the unique child they are treating? This chapter explains how to select and implement interventions that make sense given the different skill sets and personalities of each child. The sources of social impairment vary in children, and some behaviors may occur for multiple reasons. The deeper and more thoughtfully the team can consider these questions, the more likely it will be that they will select and correctly apply a strategy that yields success. Further, all team members must know how to implement the strategy correctly and understand the principles behind it so they can be flexible in the moment, modifying it in a variety of settings. Some simple strategies may take weeks to teach, and it is difficult for parents and professionals not to become discouraged. Attention to the child's team as a functioning unit is needed (see Chapter 6).

Designing a successful social intervention entails the following:

1. Identifying the target behavior.
2. Considering the child's learning profile with regard to the behavior to be taught.
3. Identifying possible strategies that may be appropriate and feasible to implement.
4. Considering whether the strategy or the new social behavior can be taught and practiced in multiple settings.
5. Anticipating problems with implementation.

Although some consider that making sure the intervention approach is evidence based or a best practice is the most critical issue, in fact, each of these components of planning is equally important. The most well-researched and established intervention will fall flat if not implemented with care.

A challenge that sets skill development for social behavior apart from teaching other kinds of behaviors is finding the right kind of motivation to induce a child to perform the behavior. Identifying motivating consequences for appropriate social behavior requires a customized plan, based on the level of social interest of the child. A child who is interested in peer interaction but just cannot seem to get it right might benefit from a visual prompt that reminds him that performing the behavior correctly will lead to improved chances of making friends. If a child has little social interest, then strategies must include reinforcements tied to highly rewarding activities or objects, and a visual cue may be needed to help the child remember the reward for correct responding. Ultimately, if social experiences are pleasurable and arousing in a positive way for the child, the experience of social interaction may become reinforcing in and of itself. This is an area of ongoing research (Lerner, Mikami, & Levine, in press; Rogers & Dawson, 2010).

IDENTIFY THE TARGET BEHAVIOR

We must prioritize which social behaviors will be targets for the intervention, based on the child's developmental level and the current social context. This process is individualized for each child, hence the phrase "designing child-specific intervention." It may be best to start with modest goals for addressing a particular social behavior, taking care to recognize the basic social skills that are needed to successfully execute the full behavior. The best way to identify the target behavior is to observe a social scenario in which the child is having trouble and to dissect the scenario in such a way as to identify the gaps in the child's social understanding and performance.

As an example, a 6-year-old child in kindergarten, with below-average receptive and expressive language, low-average cognitive skills, and a very low level of self-care skills may need a teaching approach that would be appropriate for a typically developing 4-and-a-half-year-old and may need to learn social behaviors and skills typical of a 3-year-old. Returning again to Figure 3-2, a wide variety of behaviors may be targets for intervention. These are arranged in developmental sequence to emphasize that complex social competencies are built on a foundation of more basic skills, and the child is not likely to master sophisticated competencies without a firm foundation of basic skills. In this regard, once the educational team has identified all behaviors that might be a target for intervention, two or three behaviors are selected as priorities. It is better to choose a limited number of behaviors to address initially, develop a well-thought-out and comprehensive plan for intervention, and devise careful and accurate measurement strategies than to identify 10 or more behaviors that need attention. Breaking down basic skills into even smaller skills and teaching these first is almost always necessary, and, of course, reinforcement strategies must be well thought out and tailored to the particular child and environment.

Obviously, behavior such as aggression, self-injury, and eloping from the learning environment must be a central focus of treatment if present. Working with a behavior analyst to obtain a functional assessment and/or analysis of these behaviors and developing a detailed intervention plan is probably most efficient. While social goals can and should be addressed even if these behaviors are ongoing, do not underestimate the degree to which disruptive behaviors set a child apart from peers, from the peers' point of view. Children are quite aware of their peers' behavior in the school setting and may steer clear of children who exhibit these kinds of challenging behaviors. Further, children are influenced strongly by their teachers' behavior toward a child with challenging behavior (Mikami, Lerner, & Lun, 2010).

Returning to the issue of identifying a social behavior to target for teaching, it may be appropriate to consider whether the child has not acquired the behavior—literally does not know how to do it—or has a performance deficit—that is, the child has the behavior in his repertoire but does not know when to use it (Bellini, 2008). Making this distinction helps the team become more precise in terms of thinking about how to intervene. The answer to this question will impact what strategies you choose for intervention. Again, when considering social goals and objectives and targeting social behaviors, it is best to consider the child's developmental level as a starting point for teaching skills. Teaching a fourth grade student with ASD how to interact with other fourth graders will be difficult if the target student is functioning socially on a first grade level. It may be better to start the intervention with children who are more closely matched developmentally to the target child, perhaps a bit younger than fourth grade and a bit older than first grade, to ensure some success before working toward helping the child develop more mature social behavior.

CONSIDER THE CHILD'S LEARNING PROFILE WITH REGARD TO THE SOCIAL BEHAVIOR TO BE TAUGHT

The child's cognitive profile is important to keep in mind, identifying where strengths and weaknesses lie with regard to understanding information, with the objective of exploiting strengths and supporting weaknesses as you select an intervention strategy. For example, if the child shows strength in identifying visual patterns, perhaps the social skill to be taught can be explained and practiced concretely using a series of pictures that use visual patterns to depict the skill before being practiced in a more realistic setting.

The child's language profile is important for the same reason. We must understand where strengths and weaknesses lie, again with a view toward choosing an intervention strategy that will exploit language strengths and support weaknesses. Depending on the child's language profile, we may want to use a restricted vocabulary or truncated language when implementing any of the strategies described in Chapter 5. It may be important to use repetition or allow the child extra time to respond to even the simplest of instructions, comments, or questions. If the child has weak narrative language skills, this weakness may need to be addressed intensively in one-to-one sessions with an educator, who then helps the child narrate new social experiences as he or she is exposed to them, with a view toward developing greater understanding of the social panorama and the child's place in a given social situation (L. Booth, 2011, personal communication).

Finally, when selecting target behaviors, we must identify other behavior issues, such as inattention or anxiety, that limit the child's ability to learn new skills and behaviors; these issues will need to be addressed alongside the intervention plan to help the child master new social behaviors. Comorbid symptoms will interfere with social teaching and performance and hinder the child's social development. The team may reach out to a specialty clinic for children with ASD or a professional with expertise and experience in diagnosing and treating comorbidities as a way to augment the intervention.

IDENTIFY APPROPRIATE AND FEASIBLE STRATEGIES

Consider the child's temperament and the context (classroom, playground, school psychologist's office) and select a strategy that is feasible, can be implemented logistically, and will be acceptable to the child. This does not mean that the child agrees to the strategy but rather that adults can introduce and implement the strategy as a part of the child's day in a way that the child can learn to accept. Children have varying levels of awareness of their social challenges, and this must be considered when planning an intervention. There is no need to provide a child with a detailed explanation of her social challenges. For some children, particularly younger children and those who have little awareness of their social disability, it is appropriate to incorporate the new strategy into the course of the day without any discussion. More able children may need an explanation, but it should be in the simplest terms (even for very bright children). At times, professionals make the mistake of believing that a very bright child with an ASD can understand his social disability from an intellectual point of view, without considering the child's emotional state or self-esteem. We come across many teenagers with severe social disabilities who are defensive about their vulnerabilities and are not willing to participate in learning activities. In these situations, building an alliance with children or teens, highlighting their unique (and perhaps highly unusual) personal style as a part of what makes them who they are, may be a first step. Once a trusting alliance is built, children may be willing to accept the idea of modifying their behavior to interact with others who just do not understand them.

Additionally, the team has to feel comfortable with the strategy and be clear about how to implement it. Promoting social development in school-age and teenage children is a new enterprise for school teams, and nobody can be expected to know all the strategies and details of implementation available. Talking out the details, considering the child's schedule and how other children may impact the plan, is needed ahead of time. Team members should be comfortable sharing their doubts and their concerns about the process.

Once a strategy is selected, the team may decide to teach certain skills in advance with an adult, and then practice with one trained peer, before training the child in a group situation, using visual prompts and self-monitoring strategies. The key is to help the child incorporate the behavior into her repertoire fluidly, gradually elaborating on the behavior so that it becomes flexible. As the child begins to grasp how to perform the new social behavior, issues of timing and perhaps rules about when not to engage in the behavior might need to be taught.

CONSIDER WHETHER THE BEHAVIOR CAN BE PRACTICED IN MULTIPLE SETTINGS

Once the team has implemented a teaching strategy, they should consider whether the same strategy will be used to practice the new skill in different settings, or whether a different strategy will be needed. The skill or behavior should be taught in multiple settings. It is also important to convey to the child, if the child is able to understand, whether through visuals, text, or conversation, how this newly learned behavior is working in each setting. If it is not, the interventionist can troubleshoot the problem with the child. These therapeutic activities provide a linking function—helping the child connect a social behavior in one setting to the same behavior in another setting. The goal is to help the child see the big picture, learning how a behavior can be modified and used flexibly in multiple environments. Some kids will understand this, perhaps with repetition, and others will not. For lower-functioning or nonverbal children, a visual cue that accompanies the child across settings may be useful to extend the behavior to a new context. With much practice and repetition, this may be successful.

ANTICIPATE PROBLEMS WITH IMPLEMENTATION

Since social understanding is so weak in children with ASDs, it makes sense to anticipate problems with implementation and learning. If the child engages in negative behaviors, we may see an increase in those behaviors (termed an *extinction burst*) when we implement new strategies, as the child becomes stressed and tries to escape the demands of the novel expectations for learning. Everyone on the team should be warned about this and prepared to respond to it therapeutically. Sometimes the escalation of negative behavior is so severe that team members panic or assume that the strategy is a failure. Parents in particular struggle with seeing their child in distress and may want to throw in the towel. The whole team needs to hang together through this time, to determine whether to ride through the escalation of behavior or to back off and take things more gradually. This is a judgment call that the team makes together.

Finally, it is not the case that a particular social problem or behavior is solved best with one strategy versus another. The issue is that the team must try to create a good match between the child, the context, and the strategy to reach a particular outcome. For example, if the child is learning to initiate play or join a group at play, given the child's personality and profile, the team must ask themselves: Is it best to start by watching a video, then reviewing the video with the child, role-playing with the child, and then having the child practice with facilitation on the playground? Or given the child's personality and profile, would it be better to consider using peer tutors to help with integration into play? If remembering the steps for joining in is not the child's strong suit, could some cue cards be devised (and kept out of the sight of peers) that can help him to review the process?

This brings us full circle to the challenge of helping children with ASD develop social competency. There simply is no single right way to do it, and since all children are different, competent social behavior may not always look the same for every child. Herein lies the crux of the problem. What we are truly seeking is to promote ongoing social development in children with ASD, so that as they grow physically, cognitively, and emotionally, they develop socially as well. Social development, in fact all of development, is a layered process, in which skills, behaviors, and competencies build on one another and thus become more and more integrated as the child grows. Teaching a basic behavior may not be so difficult, but helping the child integrate the behavior fluidly and correctly—bringing it into the behavioral repertoire—is as much an art as a science.

CHAPTER FIVE

Strategies for Promoting Social Development

· ·

Strategies most likely to be effective with regard to promoting social development are those that incorporate behavioral principles within a developmental framework. The following sections describe particular strategies considered best practice or evidence based, followed by guidelines for intervention. These differ from a broad-based approach as described in Chapter 2, in that they may be implemented to address a particular issue versus addressing all the core symptoms of ASD. Each section includes case examples to illustrate the way a strategy might be implemented and evaluated (always including generalization). For each, I include some—not all—of the research behind the approach. Keep in mind that there has to be a good fit between the child and the approach or strategy used.

APPLIED BEHAVIORAL ANALYSIS

Applied behavioral analysis (ABA) is a scientific field that seeks to understand how to apply behavioral principles to problems in daily life, whether these are behaviors we want to teach and encourage or those we want to eliminate and discourage. It is neither a set of instructional strategies, nor is it an educational curriculum (Strain & Schwartz, 2001). Oddly, this field is probably the best studied and the most misunderstood when it comes to intervention for children with ASD!

ABA is a theoretical model for understanding behavior and teaching new behavior based on principles of operant conditioning. Simply put, behavior that is reinforced is strengthened and behavior that is not reinforced is extinguished. This statement belies the complexity of ABA, however, since learning how behavior is learned, reinforced, maintained, and extinguished is more complicated than we might think. We must understand principles of direct teaching, how reinforcement works, what techniques are effective for modifying and shaping behavior, how generalization is promoted, and how new behaviors are maintained over time using deliberate strategies for the child within the environment. ABA is rooted in the theories and experiments of B. F. Skinner (1953) but had a huge revival in the 1960s and 1970s when Ivar Lovaas began using principles of ABA to develop highly structured strategies for teaching children with autism (McEachen, Smith, & Lovaas, 1993). Lovaas's very well-known study, published in 1987, described 19 children diagnosed with autism who had received 40 hours of intensive treatment for more than 2 years, and who made substantial gains. Even though some students made minimal gains and there were some methodological flaws in the research, parents and interventionists jumped on this highly structured method for teaching. Unfortunately, many who read or learned about Lovaas's approach applied it in a narrow way, not appreciating that the approach included carefully planned stages of intervention that included moving beyond the one-to-one, highly structured, repetitive, adult-child teaching sessions (known as discrete trial training). The UCLA Young Autism Project, based on this work, provided a comprehensive program of ABA intervention, including training for parents and paraprofessionals (often college students), intervention in the home and in school settings over time, and increased emphasis on naturalistic instruction (naturalistic settings and reinforcements) (Smith, Groen, & Wynn, 2000). The focus of this program of intervention was the development of language, social skills, and adaptive behavior. The aim was to help the children develop satisfying relationships and functional behavior in day-to-day settings.

Currently, educators, parents, and community professionals use principles of ABA when working with both typically developing children and children with disabilities. Using a reward system to teach a toddler to use the potty, praising a student for doing well on a test, or allowing children to earn an allowance are all examples of strategies employing operant teaching principles. The difference when working with children with ASDs is that these children are not as easy to motivate (they may not respond to praise, which is a social reward); the rewards that they do respond to may be hard to discover and idiosyncratic; and they may need more explicit teaching for a simple task than a typical child. Breaking down a task into its smallest components is often necessary, with direct teaching and reinforcement for learning each component. Once each component is mastered, the interventionist works with the child to chain together the behaviors to complete a sequence. Prompting and reinforcement are used initially, but then prompting is faded if possible to allow the child to flexibly perform the behavior independently.

Teaching children social skills and behavior using these principles is challenging at best, compared to teaching a task such as washing hands, getting dressed, or completing homework. Social expectations change depending on the setting, the people, and the context (e.g., play, classroom, dinnertime). Age and sex play a role in what is socially appropriate as well, and these behavioral expectations cannot be taught easily since there are so many variables at play at any one time (Koenig & Tsatsanis, 2005). Nevertheless, basic strategies such as direct teaching, prompting, reinforcing behavior (to encourage or extinguish it), chaining behaviors, fading prompts, and using these same strategies to promote newly learned behaviors in new settings may be useful for teaching social behaviors.

A straightforward example of teaching a direct behavior with prompting and reinforcement is to teach a kindergarten child to approach a group of children playing, sit nearby, and observe. The child might get a prompt to simply sit for a brief period of time and receive a desired reward for following through. This routine might be followed many times before the child is instructed to choose a toy from among those available and play alongside the other children, once again, for a designated period of time and for a reward. Over time, the child is taught, using direct instruction, prompt, and reinforcement, to share a toy or engage in a simple play sequence (with some actions and some commenting), with an adult, and then to do the same with a peer. This kind of practice in playing would be most successful if a peer were taught how to respond and reinforce the child's attempts to engage. A plan to teach and practice this strategy in multiple settings might lead toward generalization as long as there are elements in the new setting that are consistent with those from the first setting, and there is consistency with respect to prompting and reinforcement.

Strain and Schwartz (2001) described a modest literature using ABA strategies that supports the use of the following:

1. Procedures that prompt and reinforce a child for positive overtures toward peers
2. Procedures in which children are provided with toys and materials or instructions that lead to greater interaction with peers
3. Procedures in which typical children are taught specific

ways of engaging in positive interaction with children with ASD

4. Procedures in which reinforcement is provided to a group of children based on the group (and the target child) maintaining a certain level of social interaction.

In one study of preschool children, boys worked in pairs to learn and rehearse motor and language strategies to engage a child with autism in play (Strain, Shores, & Tim, 1977, cited in Strain & Schwartz, 2001). For example, they would comment, "Let's play!" and roll a ball to the target child (with ASD), who had been taught to respond with a comment or roll the ball back. Subsequent prompting in different settings led to increased interaction between the target child and peers in those settings as well. The investigators noted that one child, who had higher levels of self-stimulatory behavior and less adept social behavior prior to the intervention, made little progress. When peer tutors increased their initiations and learned how to respond to nonresponsive or self-stimulatory behavior by the target child, the result was increased social responding in the target child. A series of studies conducted by Strain and colleagues showed that peer initiations, praise, and response to the target child's initiations were correlated with increased social behavior by the child with ASD. Further, high rates of stereotypical behavior did not appear to hinder the target child's ability to respond (Strain & Schwartz, 2001). Rather, these behaviors tended to occur when the child was left to his or her own devices, without peer interactions.

The most effective strategy for peer tutors (at the preschool level) was to teach them to organize play, make suggestions, share offers and requests, offer and ask for assistance, and make general comments to the child with ASD (Strain & Schwartz, 2001). This ABA-based therapy, administered by peers, resulted in significant gains for children with ASD. More information regarding peer-mediated approaches is included later in this chapter. To implement a behavioral approach for teaching a particular social behavior, we must first break down the behavior into its smallest components. It is important to make sure that the behavior we have selected matches the child in his or her social context. For example, rarely do young children introduce themselves when approaching a new group, nor are they likely to ask, "How are you?" These are adult approaches that do not fit the social context of young schoolchildren, and they are likely to make a child stand out from peers rather than be accepted. Drs. Fred Frankel and Robert Myatt (2003) described a teaching procedure termed "slipping in," which essentially guides a child in how to join a group of children at play in a fluid way that is most likely to be accepted by the group. What is impressive about this strategy is that it acknowledges how children truly behave in social interaction versus how adults might construe a play entry strategy. Too often, when adults attempt to teach a child to play, the behaviors taught do not reflect what really happens in play.

Let's get back to using principles of ABA to teach social behavior to children with ASD. Critical for success is applying these principles systematically and, if results are not obtained, evaluating each step of the teaching plan to consider what may not be working. The following steps may be a helpful framework:

- Identify the social behavior you want the child to learn.
- Observe and describe how this behavior is performed by typically developing peers.
- Break the behavior down into as many components as possible, to make it as simple as possible to teach.
- Decide the most accurate and easy way to record whether the child performs each newly learned behavior correctly.

- Consider what motivates the child with ASD to comply with a behavioral routine. This may include conducting an assessment in which the child specifically identifies what is motivating. Select reinforcers based on this activity.
- Teach the child explicitly how to perform each component of the social behavior; prompt the child and reward attempts and successful executions of the behavior in practice with adults.
- Chain all component behaviors together, one at a time, until all are included in the sequence, and reinforce successful performance of the chained behaviors.
- Provide a guided opportunity for the child to practice the new social behavior with peers (peers may be coached ahead of time to be accepting).
- Provide multiple opportunities for the child to practice the new behavior, handle feedback, and deal with consequences, with adult support.
- Reward the child for all attempts to practice the behavior; reward peers as needed.
- Provide opportunities to practice in new settings and with new peers.
- Ensure that parents and other adults in the child's world know the procedure for prompting the child (adults should implement the procedure in a consistent way, but with some flexibility).
- Gradually fade the prompts and support any behavior on the part of the child to participate spontaneously.
- Fade reinforcements if possible.

Case Example

Susan is a 9-year-old girl, diagnosed with pervasive developmental disorder not otherwise specified. A cognitive assessment shows that Susan has nonverbal problem-solving skills in the low average range, and verbal problem-solving skills in the borderline range. Her language assessment reveals low average receptive language ability as well as below average expressive abilities. Susan has significant impairment in pragmatic language skills, including poor interpretation of nonverbal communication (e.g., gestures, facial expressions, prosody) and difficulty with turn taking and responding to comments or questions in conversation. Her adaptive play and interactive skills are at about the 6- to 7-year level. Susan is in the third grade, mainstreamed, with resource room support for math and language arts. Susan's reading decoding skills are at the second grade level, while reading comprehension is at the kindergarten level. Susan has particular difficulty interpreting the gist or gestalt of a story or social scenario, tending to focus on the details. Susan would like to make friends and spend time with other girls her age, but cannot seem to connect with these girls during recess. She is not invited to social gatherings outside of school, and although she is not aware of this, her mother is.

How can we help Susan connect with other girls her age? It makes sense to take stock of Susan's strengths and weaknesses in the cognitive and language domains and to understand what is motivating to her, whether it is tangible rewards or perhaps opportunities to engage in preferred activities. This should be done not only by asking teachers and parents what motivates her but by determining what she identifies as motivating, as these preferences are not always the same (Resetar & Noell, 2008). Next, it is important to understand what Susan understands about the social context of third grade girls, in her school and community. Observing typical children at play or during conversation will help the adults to consider what constitutes successful interaction and to understand what skills Susan lacks. It is important to consider broad behaviors and then break these behaviors down into smaller components, and to identify what foundational skills (see Figure 1-1) underlie these components. Certain foundational skills may be taught directly, as preparation for learning more complex social skills. This might include using direct teaching and reinforcement strategies to learn how to discern facial expressions, interpret a limited number of gestures, and interpret basic prosodic elements of speech. These direct teaching sessions would be carried out in a highly structured learning environment, with extensive practice, to ensure that Susan absorbs the information and can apply it in diverse contexts. Next, Susan could be guided through structured play interactions, with a facilitating adult to help her participate in the kinds of social games and interactions typical of third grade girls. The facilitator would draw teaching content from team observations regarding Susan's peer group's social interaction. Once Susan grasps some of the basics of age-appropriate social interaction, she should be provided with structured opportunities to practice interaction with one peer, preferably a child who has been coached to be a mentor. In all these social interactions and practice settings, Susan should be reinforced for correct responding. Further, her peer mentor should be reinforced, based on her own preferences, as well. As Susan and her mentor engage in multiple different scenarios for interaction, Susan should be coached by the adult facilitator and her peer mentor to expand on what she has learned to broaden her skills for social interaction.

This is a tall order for any educational team, in terms of the intensity of intervention for Susan, adult teaching, recruiting and training one or more peers, and providing guidance during social interaction opportunities with peers and then in a more general context. Nevertheless, the complexity of successful social interaction at this age requires this level of teaching and learning.

VISUAL STRATEGIES AND SUPPORTS

The use of visual strategies and supports can go a long way in helping children with ASDs understand what they are being asked to do, or communicate their needs and choices. Visual supports are photographs, line drawings, written or pictorial scripts, rule reminder cards, digital images with or without text, or text alone that cue a child to perform a behavior or make a choice (Ganz & Flores, 2008). Often, visual strategies are used to help children understand a sequence of events (an activity schedule), or to learn, remember, and perform a series of steps for completing a task (Boutot, 2009). Video modeling may also be considered a visual strategy, but because there is much detailed information about video modeling research and procedures for promoting social development, it is included in a separate section.

Visual strategies take advantage of the preference of many children with ASD for communication that does not require verbal interaction and comprehension of spoken language. Because heard information can be difficult to process and retain, visual cues, whether pictures for those who do not comprehend text, text alone for those who read and comprehend well, or a combination, can improve social communication in children with ASD. The Picture Exchange Communication System is a commercially available set of materials that has been successful in helping young children communicate with others (Ganz, Simpson, & Corbin-Newsome, 2008).

An interesting application of an activity schedule to promote social engagement was described by Betz, Higbee, and Reagon (2008). To promote social engagement, the investigators paired a preschool-age child with a child with an ASD for a play activity, which was depicted in a joint photographic activity schedule. All those participating had already learned to follow an activity schedule independently. Children had also been taught how to play simple board games with adults, so they had some practice with regard to following the rules of the game and taking turns. The joint activity schedules, which consisted of photographs depicting the steps the children would take to participate in the activities, were included in a three-ring binder, with a picture of the child designated to lead the activity at the top of the page. The role of the leader alternated between the typical child and the child with ASD. The children were taught to use the pictorial cues to proceed through a sequence of play activities. An adult facilitator worked with each group to ensure they worked together to follow the sequence, with the child leader initiating the interaction. Over time, as the children became more adept at working together to follow the play sequence, the adults increased their physical distance from the children and prompted only when the children seemed stuck (Betz et al., 2008). Finally, the adults resequenced the activities to make sure the children were learning to follow the schedule versus going through the steps of the play sequence in a rote manner. Results of this study showed that not only did the children independently complete play sequences using the activity schedule, but they continued to engage each other in interaction over time, without prompting.

Case Example

Aaron is a 13-year-old boy with strong cognitive skills and formal language skills who is diagnosed with an ASD (Asperger's disorder). Aaron is interested in politics, foreign policy, and the law, particularly the U.S. Supreme Court, and the most recent decisions and upcoming cases. He has some basic understanding of the complexity of these cases, but he tends to describe them in black and white when speaking to others and does not see the nuances of the law that are typically discussed when a case gets to the Supreme Court. At times he can discuss a case reasonably, but at other times he takes an extreme view that makes others avoid the discussion and avoid him.

Aaron wants to make friends. He sees other kids his age getting together for pizza or a movie, and he would like to be included. When he is told that his special interest in politics may not be interesting to others, he tends to argue about it, although he will eventually come around to accepting it. Yet he does not know what else to talk about, and without structure he will quickly lapse into this topic. Aaron's school team knows that although he has strong verbal skills, he may need reminders to redirect his conversation to topics of more common interest to kids his age. A couple of members of his educational team identify topics of interest to the *particular* children Aaron will be interacting with at lunch or during study hall, not topics of *general* interest to 13-year-old boys. The team plans to teach Aaron to converse, but they need to be particularly careful to tailor their training to the group of kids Aaron is trying to join. The team constructs a set of digital photographs depicting topics that Aaron might choose and elaborate on, and constructs a warning card to remind him not to divert to politics if anxious. The team may even construct a deck of cards for Aaron to use to help him cue himself to appropriate topics and also to take a break at times during conversation. This strategy could be useful, although Aaron's use of the card would need to be unobtrusive. He might select one or two cards as reminders prior to going to lunch, and then stay with those topics and rules as best he can during that lunch period. This kind of visual support is not easy to design or implement, but the degree to which it allows flexibility and self-cueing (Aaron using the cards as reminders) will promote generalization of skills and self-monitoring skills for the future.

SCRIPTS AND ROLE-PLAY

Typically developing children engage in pretend play as pre-schoolers, and it has been argued that these activities are instrumental in helping children organize their experiences and make sense of the world (Goldstein & Cisar, 1992). Teaching children scripts for interaction and using role-play to practice social interaction can be effective ways of helping children with ASD initiate, sustain, and expand social communication and play. Much of this work is based on Odom and Strain's (1984) work, which showed that children with disabilities demonstrated more social interaction during sociodramatic play than during manipulative play. To date, research findings show positive outcomes for students from preschool through adolescent years, including those with intellectual disability and limited expressive language skills (Goldstein & Cisar, 1992; Krantz & McClannahan, 1993; Krantz et al., 1998; Petursdottir, McComas, McMaster, & Horner, 2007; Reagon & Higbee, 2009). What is key when teaching scripts and helping children role-play social situations is helping children make the conversation or play their own, generalizing to different settings and people. If generalization does not occur, or the child is unable to move beyond the script or role-play scenario, the interactions feel stilted and are not likely to lead to ongoing reciprocal social communication.

Teaching a specific script for interacting with regard to toys (for preschool) or topics of common interest (adolescents) is an area of ongoing research. The majority of these studies are single-subject design or case series, in which the scripts taught are highly specific to the child with ASD (target child) and peers interacting with the child. Given the degree to which social behavior is context specific, this makes sense. Critically, the use of scripts has been particularly successful with children with intellectual disability or very limited expressive language. Further, when children learn to initiate and respond with scripting, and then elaborate their interactions with unscripted language, challenging behavior and repetitive behaviors may be reduced (Krantz & McClannahan, 1993).

Goldstein and Cisar (1992) taught specific scripts for play (magic show, pet shop, and carnival) to three triads of preschool children. Each triad consisted of two typically developing children and one child on the autism spectrum. Script training was conducted outside the classroom, and each script included three roles, so each child had some actions or comments to make during enactment. Because the children with ASD had varying levels of expressive language, the scripts were modified so that when a child with limited language enacted a role, the language in that child's script was at a manageable level. Each group needed repeated training sessions to get the play scenario correctly, and teachers prompted the children throughout the training sessions. Once trained, the children with ASD were noted to show increased social interaction with peers mostly related to the script. To assess generalization, the children's social interaction was assessed during a free-play period, and each child was paired with two different children. Two of the children with ASD also showed increased social interaction to the same level as the typical children and maintained this level of interaction during generalization. The authors concluded that learning specific scripts and role-play scenarios promoted the children's social interaction, and they noted that once children had learned one script, they learned the next two more rapidly and easily. Further, it was clear that simply providing materials to the children and having the teacher verbally describe a particular play scenario did not increase socialization. The repeated practice, with alternating roles, seemed to promote increased social interaction.

Krantz and McClannahan (1998) used a script and script-fading procedure to teach three preschoolers (ages 4 and 5 years) diagnosed with an ASD to interact with a familiar adult regarding their play activities. These children ranged from mildly to severely intellectually disabled. Each had some expressive language, essentially to make requests, but very little skill with spontaneous initiation of interaction. A premise of this study was that if the children could learn to participate in simple reciprocal exchanges, they could begin to learn to expand their verbal social communication based on adult models of interaction. As a precondition of this study, all three children knew how to use an activity schedule or picture cues to indicate what play activities they wanted to engage in. The children also were taught to read very simple text ("look" and "watch me") with instruction, modeling, and reinforcement, so they could follow text prompts embedded in their activity schedule. Once the children were adept at making these two comments, "look" and "watch me," in response to flash cards, cards with these texts were randomly embedded into the activity schedule for a particular play sequence. So a child who had selected a particular play activity would follow the sequence of play as depicted on the schedule and would also make the comment "look" or "watch me" when the textual prompt appeared in the sequence. When the children used these verbalizations, the adult would make a simple response. A considerable amount of work went into teaching the children to complete the activity schedules, including manual and verbal prompting. Over time, the children were using a 16-page activity schedule and textual cues for up to 10 activities, with no external prompting. Finally, the scripts were faded by gradually reducing the text on the activity schedule. If the children failed to use the script with a faded prompt, the full prompt was reinstituted until the child was consistently using it again. Over time, new activities were included in the schedules that did not include scripts (text cues) for interaction. The investigators found that while none of the children made any remarks to the adult during a baseline condition, all three children increased the number of initiation to adults using the script, and made spontaneous, unscripted comments to the adults following this intervention. Further, these unscripted comments occurred when using new materials and engaging in new activities that were not part of the initial training procedure. The researchers concluded that the simple texts "look" and "watch me" served as entrées to conversation that the children were able to apply to new situations.

A concern with using scripts noted by Odom & Strain (1986) is that children become dependent on adults to prompt play and conversation. These investigators suggested that embedding a visual cue within the scripted scenario may reduce prompt dependence since the visual becomes the prompt. Sarokoff, Taylor, and Poulson (2001) embedded visual prompts within conversational scripts to help two school-age children with ASD (ages 8 and 9) engage in social conversation. One child had intellectual functioning in the borderline range, and the other was mildly intellectually disabled. Both children were able to read, so conversational scripts for interaction related to either a snack or a video game were devised, and the children were taught to read their portion of the script. The visual prompt was the actual snack or the video game case, and the name of the snack or video game was repeated many times within the script. Once the children were familiar with the scripts, they were paired up for activities, and used the scripts to interact. Over time, the scripts were faded, that is, they were presented with fewer and fewer words visible. Finally, the children were presented only with the visual cue and no script. Results show that both children increased the number of unscripted statements they made to one another, and they used the scripts with novel stimuli and novel children. However, unscripted statements did not occur in these situations. Nevertheless, these children increased their verbal repertoire for interaction and learned to comment to one another on new topics. The investigators commented that the embedded visual cues were helpful in reducing reliance on the prompts, but this kind of strategy might be challenging to implement in naturalistic settings.

A basic procedure for an intervention to promote social interaction based on scripts is as follows:

- Consider the goal for the target child based on developmental level, for example, learning to initiate play, learning to participate in or increase reciprocal play, or learning to initiate, respond, and sustain conversation.
- Measure the frequency of the desired behavior in the target child prior to the intervention.
- Create a simple script to be taught to the child using verbal prompting, an activity schedule, or text prompts; teach the target child the script with an adult until mastered.
- Teach typical peers to engage in the play or conversation using the script.
- Prompt the target child and typical peers to use the script; if possible, design a visual cue as a prompt so that adults can remove themselves from the interaction.
- Measure the target child's performance with respect to the scripted interaction.
- Measure the target child's performance with regard to increased frequency of play initiations, comments, and so on that are unscripted.
- Set up situations in new contexts, with new materials (if using toys) and with new peers to promote generalization of skills (See Chapter 7).

Case Example

Nicole is a 15-year-old young woman with borderline intellectual functioning and ASD who is in the ninth grade. She is mainstreamed for academic work, with a modified curriculum and resource room support. Nicole sits at a lunch table with a couple of other students but with little to no interaction during lunch. Her team would like Nicole to engage in conversation with her peers, but have had trouble devising a strategy that does not depend on adults being very involved. The team decides to teach Nicole three simple scripts for interaction regarding (1) lunch preferences, (2) online gaming, and (3) the school play. The script topics are chosen based on what the team hears typical children in the ninth grade discussing during lunch. Further, since there is only so much that can be discussed about school lunches, the other topics are deliberately dynamic in nature, meaning that the discussion can continue over a period of days. A visual prompt depicting the topic is designed as a signal to Nicole to start the conversation. Nicole works with an adult one-on-one to learn these scripts and then practices with a peer tutor in a private setting. She then sits with her peer tutor at her lunch table; her tutor places the visual prompt on the table; and the two carry on a conversation. Note that the visual prompt could be a magazine about online gaming or a flyer about the school play. They invite comments from others at the lunch table and respond to comments made by others. Over time, Nicole appears more comfortable in conversation with her peer tutor and begins to make unscripted comments and ask novel questions.

This example presents the ideal outcome for a student using a script procedure and with a peer tutor. Problems could include Nicole adhering rigidly to the script and appearing artificial in conversation, or needing continued learning of new scripts to maintain conversations. If the latter occurred, the team might have to revisit whether, given Nicole's ASD, she is able to learn more spontaneous conversation, or whether the intervention may be simply to provide her with as many scripts as she can manage in order to make some social connections. She might also need more time to become less scripted, for example, taking several months to reach that point instead of days or weeks. Depending on her level of functioning, Nicole may be able to generalize this skill to new settings, or her team might need to devise visual prompts to get her started in new settings for a time. Modifications can be made to support Nicole's learning, but always with the goal of helping her make the skill her own and reducing prompt dependency.

DEVELOPMENTAL PLAY APPROACH

Most contemporary approaches to intervention use play as a medium for teaching new social skills and behaviors to children with ASD. The degree to which the intervention is fashioned around the child's play interests depends on the child's learning profile and learning needs, and often on whether interventionists know how to use play scenarios to teach social behavior and help the child become socially competent across settings and people (Boutot, Guenther, & Crozier, 2005). In this section, the Integrated Play Group (IPG) model is described (Wolfberg, 2009) as an example of an intervention model that relies heavily on teaching children with ASD to engage in functional and symbolic play, in the context of peer interaction and facilitated guidance from adults.

Wolfberg and Schuler (1999) reported on three children, all age 7 years and diagnosed with an ASD, who participated in IPGs. The children participated in these groups with nondisabled peers. The IPG model for intervention includes the following:

1. Natural, integrated settings
2. Well-designed play spaces (i.e., spatial organization of the room and access to play materials)

3. Play materials selected based on their interactive potential and complexity
4. A consistent routine for the play
5. Play groups that include typical children
6. A focus on the child's ability to initiate interaction at any developmental level, even if the behavior is idiosyncratic
7. Adult-guided participation
8. Full immersion in play

The last item refers to the fact that children are involved in every aspect of play, whatever their capabilities. Unusual behaviors may be incorporated into the play as a way to promote the child's interest.

In this study, the children's behavior was measured over the course of 7 months of intervention in the IPG. The play groups were 30 minutes in length, twice weekly. Investigators measured rates of involvement in play and interviewed parents and teachers to obtain qualitative information regarding the child's play behavior. Following baseline measurements, which revealed little interactive play between the target children and peers, adults facilitated interaction between the target children and their peers in a systematic way, helping the children move from isolated play to play with awareness of, and orientation toward, other children. Results showed that the children increased their time playing with toys appropriately and engaging in more interactive forms of play. Children also showed increases in symbolic play with toys as well as more social play with peers. The investigators concluded that guided participation in functional and symbolic play, in the context of a peer group, resulted in more engaged and elaborate play on the part of the children with ASD. Outstanding questions were how level of language and communication competence and the presence of peers influenced outcome.

Yang, Wolfberg, Wu, and Hwu (2003) described two chil-

dren, ages 6 and 7 years, diagnosed with ASD, who participated in integrated play groups with typically developing peers.
The intervention was based on the IPG model, which again pre-
sumes role-play is a means for children to develop understanding of their social and cultural context, and that contextual elements (e.g., visual supports) help children communicate with
others in their environment to progress toward designated
goals. The adult facilitator monitored play initiations, provided scaffolding for play, provided guidance with respect to
communication attempts and strategies, and provided guidance about the play, helping the child with ASD step up and
meet challenging, but manageable, expectations. Based on direct observation and parent and peer interviews, the target
children made gains in social and symbolic play. Parents reported that these gains were generalized to other settings, although this was not measured by direct observation.

A modified, integrated play group intervention was implemented with twin brothers with autism, age 6 years, using
three peer tutors who had been taught to use IPG strategies to
guide the play (Zercher, Hunt, Schuler, & Webster, 2001). During a training phase for the tutors, they identified and practiced play scenarios, using toys and props, and learning scripts
for different play themes. Further, they learned to facilitate
play through cueing the target children in what to do and what
to say during the play and coaching the children to initiate,
respond to initiations, maintain interactions, and stay involved
in the play. During weekly play sessions for 20 weeks, the adult
trainers provided support to the tutors but did not interact
with the target children. During the last 5 weeks, the tutors
carried out the intervention independently, without coaching
from the adult facilitators. The tutors adhered well to the
training strategies they had been taught during the intervention. The target children showed increased frequency of joint
attention behaviors, symbolic play, and language use. One

child showed increased social initiation during the intervention while the other did not. This study incorporated developmentally appropriate play opportunities for two children with autism, as well as the use of scripts and peer tutors. The tutors constructed the play scenarios in the final phase of intervention, based on their interests and what they perceived the target children to be interested in. In this way, the play sessions were quite naturalistic, including toys and games all the children liked, and having peers take the lead in engaging the children with autism. A very similar study by Ganz and Flores (2008) showed improvement in commenting related to play versus making unrelated comments in two preschool children diagnosed with ASD.

Another approach to providing social learning through developmental play groups is the SCERTS program (Social Communication, Emotional Regulation, and Transactional Supports). This program, developed for preschool and school-age children is based on the work of Barry Prizant and Amy Wetherby, who designed a model for intervention that incorporates practices of contemporary ABA within a developmental framework. The three components of the model are:

- Social communication, which includes teaching joint attention skills and the capacity for symbol use and symbolic behavior.
- Emotional regulation, the ability to use sensory, motor, or cognitive and language strategies to modulate emotional and behavioral states, and the ability to use others for the same purposes, and further the ability to down-regulate once overaroused or upset.
- Transactional support, which is the use of visuals or organization supports or interpersonal, family, and professional support to manage challenging situations.

While many underlying components of the program are based on research on promoting communication skills through incidental teaching and socially valid contexts (Prizant, Weatherby, Rubin, & Laurant, 2003), and target joint attention and symbolic representation in interactions and play, the model as a whole has not been subjected to rigorous testing. Nevertheless, there is a strong emphasis on children with ASD learning in naturalistic contexts, as they interact with peers and other community members. SCERTS does not insist that all learning takes place in the context of small social groups with peers. There is room for social teaching with an adult, but the aim is for the child to develop competency to then carry out more informal interaction with peers. Teaching play skills, such as teaching children to initiate and participate in social routines and events, is emphasized (http://www.scerts.com/docs/). Again, to date there is not enough data to support the use of the model in total to address social development in children with ASDs, although the assumptions about how children learn, the premises for intervening, and the strategies for intervening are based on the general research literature in intervention in ASD amassed in the last 20 years. At least two large-scale studies are underway at present, testing the effectiveness of the model applied in its entirety.

Another model that includes child-focused play sessions aimed at learning social communication skills is Prelinguistic Milieu Teaching, which is part of a broader program, Responsivity education/prelinguistic milieu teaching (Warren et al., 2008; Yoder & Stone, 2006). The full model includes strategies for training parents to help their children learn social communication (covered later in this chapter), but is explained in brief here as an example of using play sessions to teach social communication to children with ASDs. In play sessions, the therapist works one on one with a child to establish play routines, or sequences using a toy or activity, until the child becomes highly motivated to communicate (Yoder & Warren, 1998). The therapist engages the child in multiple routines and then holds back, giving the child a chance to signal that he or she would like the activity to continue. The therapist may use a physical prompt to get the child to look and make a request for the activity. Once the child can follow through with this activity consistently, the therapist moves to more complex forms of communication, including drawing the child's attention to an object or activity (establishing joint attention routines). In one study, Yoder and Warren (1998) found that the degree to which children develop responsive communication with adults and peers depended as much on how interactive and responsive parents were at home as on whether children practiced social interaction skills with an adult one to one or with a small group composed of an adult and peers. This speaks to the need for parent involvement in intervention to promote social interaction, as well as the need to teach social interaction skills in school and in practice with peers.

Designing play groups is best done by attending to a very specific model for intervention, whether it be those mentioned above or other groups with some evidence base emerging in the research literature. At the very least, interventionists must consider these factors:

- The importance of a naturalistic environment, with toys appropriate to the developmental level of the child, and possibly some toys below the child's developmental level to allow a child to demonstrate mastery.
- The mix of typically developing children to those with special needs as a means to maximize modeling and interaction.
- The degree to which adult facilitators will direct the play, by introducing themes or scripts, or by allowing the children to develop their own themes, to the extent that they can.

- The methods for helping children manage their level of arousal and possible conflict with the other children.
- The need to structure the play session so that it ends successfully every time.

Case Example

Charlie, age 3 years, 1 month, has recently enrolled in preschool in his public school district following a transition from early intervention. Charlie's developmental testing suggests he is delayed relative to same-age peers in terms of problem solving and receptive and expressive language. His adaptive skills are delayed as well, in that he is not toilet trained, as are the majority of the children in his preschool class, he cannot dress himself (coat on and off), does not sit for circle time or snack, and does not interact with the other children. Charlie spends his time in solitary and repetitive play, flipping pages of books, dropping items from a table, peering at string or yarn as he shakes it, and pulling toys he wants out of other children's hands. Charlie's team is quite adept at creating structure to help Charlie follow the preschool routine, in terms of morning activities, hanging up his coat, and so on, and sitting for morning circle time (even though they know he gets little out of it). In general, they are experienced enough to know how to structure his day to help him move through the planned activities without an outburst. Nevertheless, they want to see him more engaged with peers, to promote naturalistic interaction and play. Charlie does relate to adults, but only to signal his needs and wants, and minimally at that.

Charlie's team wants to help him to orient toward his peers and look to them for satisfying interactions. At present, he seems satisfied with stereotypic play. Since he has little tolerance for interactions with his peers, it seems risky to try to include him in even a small play group. The team decides that Charlie's speech-language pathologist, Laura, will work with him one on one in brief play sessions to help him (1) attend to the activity, (2) attend to her directives, (3) wait for her verbal comments and cues, and (4) follow through with the activity as prescribed. Laura uses heightened affect, through facial expressions and verbalizations, to increase Charlie's level of arousal and help him feel motivated to engage in the interaction. Over the course of 12 sessions, Laura stays consistent with this routine until Charlie can follow the play activities, with turn taking and attending to his play partner. As time goes on, she slowly modifies the routine to modify and expand the play, moving forward as Charlie tolerates changes and backing off if any change seems too upsetting.

Once Laura and the team feel that Charlie is doing well with this routine, they expand the intervention to include one other child from Charlie's class. The play with this child is highly structured by the adult and very much focused on helping Charlie and his peer master the social developmental tasks appropriate to 3½-year-old children. In this regard, the children and the interventionist go over the play activities again and again, until both children have the routines for play completely embedded in their repertoire. While some might suggest that this rote adherence to play routines might not lead to spontaneous play, it is actually a necessary entrée into activities that include spontaneous and elaborate play. Once again, as Charlie and this peer (and other peers) perform these play activities competently, the group facilitators present more complex play and introduce new players. All of this is done thoughtfully and systematically, guided by the notion that Charlie needs to expand his play skills over time, but that this expansion needs to be paced in such a way that he is not overwhelmed. This balance is critical for all interventions that aim to integrate children with ASD into settings with typically developing peers. The upsetting or jarring effect of new people and activities presented too abruptly to children with ASDs learning to play in a group cannot be overemphasized.

VIDEO MODELING

Video modeling is a strategy for teaching many kinds of skills, including daily living, community, and social skills. In its simplest form, the intervention involves videotaping a model performing a behavior to be learned, such as making a bed, looking both ways before crossing a street, or joining a group of first graders playing a game at recess. The premise is that the child with ASD may learn the new behavior by seeing it demonstrated repeatedly by another. There is good evidence to suggest that video modeling may be an effective teaching tool and that we have yet to exploit its possibilities. However, the current research base raises as many questions as it answers (Apple, Billingsly & Schwartz, 2005; Ayres & Langone, 2005; Charlop & Milstein, 1989; LeBlanc et al., 2003; Litris, Moore, & Anderson, 2010; Nikopoulos & Keenan, 2007; Schreibman & Ingersoll, 2000; Sherer et al., 2001; Taylor, Levin, & Jasper, 1999). A review of the strategies used and the outstanding questions will help the reader figure out what might work and what might not if employing this strategy for a particular child.

Modeling as a strategy for learning is based on the work of Albert Bandura, which suggested that watching a person receive a reward for a particular behavior would increase the likelihood that the observer would model that same behavior (Sherer et al., 2001). This concept has been demonstrated numerous times with animals and people for the last 50 years. Two issues, however, are that children with ASD do not usually learn to model intuitively, and that they are less likely to be motivated by a reward that would reinforce a typical child.

These issues would have to be addressed before using a video modeling strategy with a child.

A number of investigators have pointed out the strengths of using video as a teaching tool for children and teens with ASD:

- Most children and teens enjoy television, videos, and movies.
- The video medium is likely to grab children's attention and help them avoid extraneous distractions.
- This medium might reduce a child's anxiety because minimal real-time social interaction is required.
- This strategy might tap into visual strengths that many children with ASDs have.
- The video can be used repetitively with little effort, if necessary.
- A number of modifications and elaborations can be made over time.

In one of the most successful studies of the video modeling strategy, Charlop-Christy, Le, and Freeman (2000) showed that children with ASD could be taught to greet others spontaneously, engage in play activities, learn language, and generalize some of these skills. The investigators highlighted that children must have the prerequisite skill of imitation and ability to attend to multiple salient cues and screen out nonrelevant visual and auditory information. Thus, children might need specific direct instruction with repeated practice on these skills prior to participating in a video modeling strategy.

Sherer and Pierce (2001) used a video modeling strategy to teach five children with ASD and developmental delay, age 7 years, to comment and respond to comments during different play scenarios. The investigators generated a number of scripts and trained the children with ASD to engage in these scripts with a typically developing peer. The children with ASD were actively prompted during the procedure, while being video-taped. Next, the investigators edited the adult prompting activities out, so that the children would view themselves commenting and responding to questions. After a period of weeks, three children showed an increased ability to independently respond to the comments without any kind of prompting. Two children did not show any increased responding, even after more than 50 training sessions. Further, when new questions were used to test generalization, the children who had learned to respond during the test phase did less well. The investigators speculated that the children who did well had strengths in verbal memory, but this was not formally tested.

As in every other strategy we use to teach children with ASD to be socially responsive, generalization is the key. Without effort to extend the learning across contexts and people, even the most perfect performance on a task has little meaning. In a study to teach perspective taking, three children ages 7 to 13 years with ASD (and with mental age equivalents of 5, 6, and 15 years) were shown a video of a classic perspective-taking paradigm, the Smarties task (LeBlanc et al., 2003). In this paradigm, the child views person A with a box of candy, while another (person B) looks on. When person A leaves the room, person B replaces the candy with something else, sealing the box as before. Person A returns to the room and the child is then asked what person A thinks is in the box (which is labeled Smarties). Children who lack perspective-taking skills will not understand that someone who did not observe the candy being replaced will still think the candy is in the box.

In the experiment, children were shown a videotape of an adult going through the Smarties scenario, and the video was paused to ask the children what was happening, to assess their ability to take perspective. The investigators trained the children repeatedly until all could answer the questions correctly.

At a follow-up test 1 month later, two of the three participants could pass the test, even when the investigators varied the materials and asked novel questions (LeBlanc et al., 2003). In this study, it is not clear that the children could apply perspective-taking concepts in real life or social situations, only that they were trained to task in a very concrete way. It was also not clear why one child did not do as well as the other two. Since perspective-taking skills develop in typical children between the ages of 3 and 4 years, was it realistic to expect the child with ASD and a mental age of 5 years to learn this skill? After all, the end point of learning perspective taking is to apply it conceptually in relationships, not in concrete tasks.

Apple et al. (2005) implemented a video modeling strategy in combination with a self-management strategy to teach two children with ASD to compliment one another in social situations. The investigators chose typically developing peers (based on teacher recommendations) to act in videos, which were about 1 minute in length. An adult narrated some instructions regarding compliment giving during the video, and multiple videos (exemplars) were shown. Following viewing, the target children were observed during free play to monitor any increased initiation or compliment giving, but none was observed. Finally, the teacher offered a reward to the child to perform the behavior, and peers were coached to approach the child to provide an opportunity for the target child to initiate. This strategy worked best. When rewards were removed, one child continued to compliment other kids, while the other did not.

To see if the children could be motivated to perform these conversational initiations, the investigators added a self-monitoring strategy. One child used a wrist counter and the other a checklist to self-report when they initiated with other children. With the addition of this strategy, both children increased initiations to others. Here, it isn't possible to separate the effects of the video modeling strategy from those of the self-monitoring strategy. The investigators suggested, however, that the use of multiple exemplars helped the students to learn the compliment-giving behavior in a more flexible way.

Video modeling appears to be most successful when investigators combine this strategy with other evidence-based strategies such as ABA, self-monitoring, peer tutoring and mentoring, and perhaps social stories (Darden-Brunson, Green, & Goldstein, 2010; Gena, Couloura, & Kymissis, 2005; Litris et al., 2010). Most important is matching the lesson to be learned via video modeling to the child's chronological and developmental level, receptive and expressive language abilities, and current play skills as well as motivation strategies meaningful to the child.

An excellent example of using video modeling to teach complex social behavior was designed by Nikopoulos and Keenan (2003), who selected three children diagnosed with ASD for the intervention, all 6 years old. All children had some language and echolalia, and all engaged in a fair amount of restricted and repetitive behaviors. The investigators selected peer models who were trained to show initiation behavior, and the videos were no longer than 30 seconds. Prior to introducing the video modeling strategy, the investigators ascertained that the children could sit and attend to a video for at least a minute and that the children had imitation skills. The target children watched the video two or three times a day, for about 5 minutes each time (several videos were shown, with different aspects of play behavior) in which the peer model approached the adult experimenter and said, "Let's play," taking the experimenter by the hand to lead him or her to some toys. Together, the peer model and experimenter played for about 10 seconds. Once this sequence was learned, the target children were taught other aspects of social play via video modeling. Ultimately, all target children learned to complete a sequence of social activities to engage another person in play. The investigators noted that while some children improved after 9 or 10 video teaching sessions, others needed 30 or more sessions to grasp and enact the social scenario. There was some evidence that the children generalized some of the initiation and play skills to other settings.

Overall, fairly strong evidence suggests that video modeling strategies, applied thoughtfully and customized to the child's learning profile and the particular context, may be quite successful in helping children develop new social behaviors. Important points to remember are the following:

- The child must have imitation skills (motor and vocal depending on what is going to be taught).
- The child must be able to attend to a video for at least 60 seconds, even if reinforcement is required to make that happen.
- The skill to be taught must be broken into its most basic components.
- It may be helpful to teach a simple, concrete task rather than a social task at first, to test the child's ability to understand the learning strategy.
- Consider the child's developmental level when selecting social behaviors for learning.
- Peers are probably preferable as models in the videos rather than adults.
- Make sure that social behaviors selected for teaching are valid for that child and that social context.
- Be prepared for the fact that many repetitions of the video may be necessary.
- For challenging behavior, filming the target child before, during, and after challenging behavior, and then editing out the challenging behavior and showing that video to the child can promote behavioral change.

Case Example

Adam is a 7-year-old boy diagnosed with ASD with borderline intellectual functioning and below-average receptive and expressive language skills commensurate with his intellectual levels. He is in the second grade, in a mainstream classroom, with resource room pull-out, as well as a paraprofessional available to support him for reading and math lessons, as well as to help him function socially in the classroom, at lunch, and on the playground. Adam's interest in other children his age is variable; he can be very interested if they are talking about his favorite cartoons (which are typically geared toward the preschool level, including Bob the Builder and Dora the Explorer) but less interested if the conversation is about karate class or soccer. He tends to walk away when the topic does not interest him, and other kids isolate him when he begins to talk about cartoons. Adam's paraprofessional tries to encourage and coach Adam to ask questions of the other children about their interests, but he either gets angry at her or asks the question and walks away before he hears the answer. Not only does he have no awareness of how his behavior appears to others, but he does not understand the reciprocal nature of conversation. That is, if he chats about karate for a bit, another child might be willing to listen to a funny story from a cartoon he likes. Adam wants to have friends, but his ideas about interpersonal relationships and his coping skills are at about the 3- to 4-year level according to the Vineland Adaptive Behavior Scales. Thus, he has minimal ability to understand his paraprofessional's explanation of why he should stay engaged in conversation with the other kids, and low frustration tolerance for listening to what other kids are saying if they are not on his topic.

Adam's school team chooses a video modeling strategy to help Adam develop the skill of conversational volley on a simple level. They begin using two peer models of Adam's age, sitting on a floor and engaging in a simple conversation (six conversation volleys at the most) about a cartoon that they both like. A second video shows the same boys talking about a cartoon, and then talking about other TV shows. A third video shows the boys talking about TV and then baseball. In each video, the boys wrap up by saying to each other, "I'm glad we're friends."

The team might begin by assessing Adam's willingness to watch the videos and providing a desired reinforcement if he appears resistant. Once this is in place, Adam watches the three videos daily before recess, with no other intervention yet. Next, a team member asks Adam to work with one of the peers to create a video and have a short conversation about cartoons and one other topic. Adam can even be prepped about the other topic so he knows what replies or comments to make. Adam and his peer may enact this scene several days in a row, with praise for doing it correctly. Next, he watches these videos right before recess. Finally, Adam might be asked to be part of a video in which there is scripted conversation, with some talk on his own interest and some talk about the other child's interests. If he becomes frustrated or stuck with this task, he is prompted to keep going, and his expressions of frustration and upset are edited out. Adam can watch himself coping well with the situation and talking (briefly) with his peer confederates on video repeatedly until he gets accustomed to this routine. Over time, team members and paraprofessionals can introduce new topics (perhaps more age-appropriate cartoons or videogames) for the boys to talk about, as a way to help Adam expand his repertoire of conversational topics.

As you can see, this is not a brief or easy intervention to implement. It could likely go on for weeks and proceed in fits and starts as Adam becomes accustomed to this new set of behaviors. However, the long-term gains, if Adam is able to learn to talk to others about their interests and allow topic switching in the service of making a friend, will be well worth it.

PEER-MEDIATED APPROACHES

Peer-mediated approaches are those that employ typically developing children to engage a child with an ASD as a means to promote that child's social behavior (Laushley & Heflin, 2000; Odom & Strain, 1986; Paul, 2003). The word *tutor* most frequently denotes a person who teaches a specific skill to another, while *mentor* describes a trusted friend, counselor, or teacher. The current research literature includes both terms, often interchangeably.

In school settings, the law requires that children with ASD be educated in the least restrictive environment to ensure exposure to their typically developing peers. However, simply providing proximity to typical children does not promote social development and social reciprocity skills in children with ASD (Odom & Strain, 1984). Affected children make the most of interaction with typical children when they and their typical peers are guided in the interaction. Further, school staff and other interventionists can modify the context to promote greater peer acceptance, social interaction, and generalization of skills. The teacher's level of acceptance of the child with ASD and the expectation that the child will be included in social activities strongly influences how the typically developing children respond to the affected child (Mikami et al., 2010).

Peer tutors are children who have been trained to engage with the target child, and the level of training may vary, depending on the age of the children and the focus of the intervention. Classroom-wide interventions, with all children participating, have shown positive effects, as have triads (two typical children and one child with ASD) and dyads (Goldstein & Cisar, 1992; Goldstein, Kaczmarek, Pennington, & Shafer,

1992; Kamps & Garrison-Harrell, 1997; Pierce & Schreibman, 1997).

Gumpel and Frank (1999) showed that using peer tutors helped socially rejected children develop positive social interaction skills. A study incorporating class-wide peer tutoring for teaching children with attention-deficit/hyperactivity disorder showed improvements in first through fifth grade students' academic performance, as well as classroom behavior in terms of activity level, engagement in the task, and off-task behavior (DuPaul et al., 1998). In a study on the effects of peer tutoring on four socially rejected boys, more frequent positive interactions were noted for all four boys (Spence, 2003). What was unusual about this study was that the target children were two kindergarten students, and the tutors were two socially rejected sixth graders. The tutors participated in an adult-mediated training during which they learned skills such as self-monitoring. All four boys made gains. The challenge when working with children with ASD is that the social reinforcement that usually provides motivation for behavior maintenance or change may not be effective with these children. Nonetheless, it may be sufficiently motivating for some children.

In a preschool setting, Goldstein and Cisar (1992) paired two typically developing children with one child with ASD to form a triad. The children had receptive and expressive language in the 3-year range, although they were from 3 to 5 years of age. Three triads were constructed; all the children with ASD had low rates of interaction with peers. The adult trainers taught all the children verbal scripts and behavioral sequences for three pretend play scenarios. Each scenario had three roles, so each child would have a part in the play. The children were taught for 15 minutes a day, and each child of the triad learned all the roles, guided by prompts. Trainers adjusted the language and sophistication of the scripts based on the developmental level of the target child. This continued until each child could enact at least 80% of each role independently. Trainers then observed the children for free play periods and noted that the number of play behaviors related to the theme increased during these periods, and the frequency of social behavior related to the theme and unrelated to the theme increased for the children with ASD. In this scenario, the play was very structured and scripted, and the adults prompted very consistently. It is not clear whether the increased social interaction behavior generalized over time to other play scenarios or with other children.

Wolfburg's model of integrated play groups for preschoolers, described previously under Developmental Play Approaches, relies heavily on peer relationships to promote social interaction in children with ASDs.

A classroom-wide intervention tested with kindergarten children showed positive effects for two 5-year-old students of average intelligence diagnosed with ASD (Laushey & Heflin, 2000). The intervention consisted of buddy training in which all children in the kindergarten class learned about how people are alike and different, using the teacher and trainer as models for demonstrating similarities and differences. The training included information about how children can choose friends based on similarities or differences, and then they were introduced to the buddy system. Each child's name was printed on an index card, and each day children were paired with a new buddy. The instructions were to "stay with your buddy, play with your buddy, and talk with your buddy." The children understood the expectations during buddy time, which was about 15 minutes in length. Reinforcement procedures were initiated, then dropped because they were not needed. Over time, the children with ASD increased their social behaviors, including asking for objects or responding, appropriately getting the attention of another, waiting for a turn, or looking at the child speaking to them, by a substantial amount. The investigators suggested that training all children helped the target children get used to interacting with different personalities and styles, similar to what they would encounter in their daily lives.

Pierce and Schreibman (1995) showed positive effects with a peer-mediated intervention using natural reinforcement and environmental modifications to increase social interaction in elementary students. In this study, two 10-year-old boys were trained through modeling, direct instruction, and role-play on how to interact with two students with ASDs (both with intellectual disability) to elicit communication. After several weeks of intervention, the children with ASD were interacting more frequently, including initiating conversation with others. One of the two children showed this behavior when paired with an untrained peer (a measure of generalization). A second study by these investigators showed positive effects for two boys ages 7 and 8, with borderline and mild impairment on intellectual testing respectively (Pierce & Schreibman, 1997). In that study, eight typically developing children were trained to use direct instruction, role-play, and modeling and feedback to promote increased social behavior in the target children. Once the intervention began, the children with ASD increased their social initiation when interacting with peers who had not yet been trained, thus showing generalization effects.

Carter and colleagues (Carter, Cushing, Clark, & Kennedy, 2005; Carter, Cushing, & Kennedy, 2009; Carter & Hughes, 2005) have documented positive effects of peer-mediated intervention with adolescents with intellectual disabilities. Interventions ranged from assigning buddies to the teen for a period of free time or assigning one or more peers to work with the target student on a project. Hughes et al. (2002) instructed typical teenagers to interact with a student with autism "as a friend" during leisure activity. This increased social interaction and the target student's communication behaviors. It is important to note that many of the studies conducted with adolescents focused on students with intellectual disability.

Typically developing children who are trained in specific strategies for interacting with children with ASD are more likely to be effective in helping kids learn and practice social behaviors than those who are not trained. Campbell (2006) showed that when typical kids learned descriptive information about the child they would be working with, including information about the target child's likes, dislikes, and personality, as well as explanatory information (meaning basic information about ASD), they were more likely to have positive feelings and thoughts about the child. Further, typical children were more likely to agree to interact with the child with ASD when they had this information.

Barron and Foot (1991) compared the outcomes of "nonelaborate" versus "elaborate" training provided to tutors prior to the peer-tutoring sessions. Nonelaborate training entailed explaining the rules and procedures necessary for carrying out the task to be taught while elaborate training included not only that but the underlying rules of the task acquisition as well. The target child's performance and the quality of interactions between the tutors and targeted children were measured. Children who had worked with the tutors who had elaborate training performed better on the task, and interactions were of a higher quality as well. Thus, the more comprehensive the training of the peer tutors, the more beneficial the tutoring seems in terms of social interactions.

Goldstein and colleagues (1992) used posters during the demonstration and training phase as well as lecture-type presentation and role-playing of each specific strategy. Koenig et al. (2010) trained tutors using a PowerPoint presentation and booklet, which explained some of the ways children with ASD experience the world. Further, the tutors were given specific concrete guidelines for interacting with the target children, as well as instructions about when to seek assistance from an adult (Figure 5-1). Peer tutors were trained to prompt and re-inforce desired behaviors.

Peer tutors are typically developing children of about the same age as the children with ASD or slightly older. If peer tutors are much older than the target child, for example, a 14-year-old teen serving as a tutor, a 10-year-old child will not view this teen as a peer, thus defeating the purpose of having the children learn to interact with peers. The main criteria for peer tutors are that they are interested in participating in the experience, they understand that they have a special role, and they are able to cope with the behaviors of the target child. Campbell (2006) noted that the best peer tutors are those that are socially adept or who have reasonable social skills but are at the periphery of their social group (e.g., classroom). Children who have been in the position of being socially rejected by peers are less competent for this sort of task.

Odom and Strain (1984) described a "fatigue effect" that might occur if peer tutors are expected to stay actively engaged over time and in different settings. If peer tutors become tired of the role, they may initate less to the target child, thus re-ducting the effect of intervention. In other words, after some time peer tutors get tired of working and stop trying as hard. To prevent that from happening, Odom suggested using some incentives or reinforcements for the peer tutors. Social praise or soft drinks at the end of work were reported to work well.

To implement a peer mentoring or tutoring program, it is important to consider the following issues:

- Does the target child have basic foundational skills, such as imitation and joint attention skills? Children who have not learned to imitate will need structured teaching, prompting, and reinforcement to benefit from peer modeling; once imi-

Children with autism spectrum disorders can:

- Have trouble understanding language, especially if sentences are complicated.

  Keep language simple.

- Have trouble understanding things they can't see, like "yesterday" or "next week."

  Use pictures to teach things that are hard to think about abstractly.

- Have difficulty knowing whether their voice is too loud or too soft.

  Tell children directly that they are speaking too loudly or too softly.

- Have trouble with touching other children when they should keep their hands to themselves.

  Tell the child the rule "keep your hands on your own body."

- May ask the same questions or say the same things over and over.

  Sometimes we might answer the question repeatedly. Sometimes we will try to ignore it to see if the child will stop. Often we try to give the child something else to say.

- May get distracted by things that others think are unimportant.

  Tell the child to do what others are doing.

- May not look other people in the face when others are speaking.

  Ask the child to look at you.

- May get frustrated more easily than other kids their age.

  The group leaders will try to identify what situations make the kids frustrated, and then change the situation to make it easier for them to handle. We figure out ways to help children gain control over their behavior if they are losing it.

Figure 5-1. Information and instructions for peer tutors.

tation skills are in place, they may be able to follow the model without more explicit structure.

- What kinds of social interaction skills are most appropriate to the target child's developmental level? This may not be consistent with chronological age.
- What peers might be available to act as tutors?
- How much structured time will be available on a regular basis for teaching and coaching the tutors? What reinforcements are possible for these children?
- How will the effect of the tutoring be measured? By using frequency of social initiations or social responses? By using length of social interaction (how many exchanges between children) or other measures?
- How will generalization of the social interaction skill be promoted and then evaluated?
- What is the projected time frame for intervention before considering whether the tutoring is helping?
- Does it make sense to describe the peer tutoring intervention to the child with ASD, or is it more appropriate to simply describe the activities in which the child will participate?

Case Example

Harrison is an 11-year-old boy diagnosed with an ASD without intellectual disability, in fact, with superior intellectual functioning. Harrison is in a mainstream fifth grade classroom, where he does well academically but rarely engages in social interaction. He answers a question when asked but generally does not ask questions, nor does he make comments to peers. His parents say that when he is pulled into an extended family activity, Harrison seems to enjoy himself, but does not initiate with others spontaneously. They also describe delays in his self-care skills, play skills, and gross motor skills. Harrison needs reminders for bathing, brushing his teeth, and wearing clean clothes. He has never engaged in or enjoyed pretend play, preferring solitary activities such as building with Legos or having screen time. Harrison can be overly rigid when playing games, to the point that he screams and leaves the game if things do not go exactly as he expects. Further, he is not able to ride a bike and does not seem to enjoy outdoor activities except for jumping on a trampoline. Harrison's parents and teachers would like to see more social interaction and activity for him during school and nonschool hours.

Harrison's team decides to try a peer tutoring strategy with Harrison and typically developing children. Because Harrison's social competency is so delayed relative to peers, they select three children from the fifth grade who are socially competent but closer in developmental terms to Harrison's level— meaning children who enjoy play and interaction similar to that which Harrison enjoys. Thus, Harrison's tutors are not athletically inclined children focused on team-oriented, competitive games, but rather children who are comfortable with building activities, for example. Two members of the team meet with potential tutors to explain the activity and gauge their interest. Three peers agree to be involved, and they attend four practice sessions to learn how to engage Harrison. The tutors learn to initiate conversation and invitations to play, reinforce Harrison's responses, and suggest play that interests Harrison. The tutors learn to seek assistance from an adult if Harrison is screaming or acting out. Once the children are comfortable with these behaviors, a team member arranges regularly scheduled play opportunities for a predetermined length of time (20 minutes, four times per week) and facilitates the social interaction. The adult prompts the peers to engage Harrison initially but fades the prompting over time as the peers do the work. Everyone is encouraged to relax and have fun.

As Harrison and the peers develop their play, team members coach the peers to expand the play to broader themes and activities. The peers use prompting and reinforcement (praise) to keep Harrison involved. Separately, Harrison works with the occupational therapist to develop bike-riding skills so he will be ready when the time comes to join his friends for a bike ride.

After several months of this kind of play, Harrison's team begins to involve new peers, asking the first group of peer tutors to coach the others about how to keep Harrison involved. Harrison's mother arranges a play date for Harrison, of limited duration and with preestablished structure and clear guidelines for Harrison in terms of behavior. If this is successful, these experiences can be replicated, and if not, Harrison's mother can discuss with team members what seemed to go well and what did not, as a way to troubleshoot and modify the intervention.

TECHNOLOGY-BASED INSTRUCTION

Over the last 15 years perhaps, technological advances have begun to make an impact on intervention for those with ASD, related to general day-to-day functioning as well as social interaction. The use of timers, pagers, cell phones, computer-based education, wrist counters, television and video, Internet applications, and Bluetooth applications have proved useful for promoting learning. While many of these applications are new and need further refinement, it is worth it to understand what might be available in the future or how current technologies might be applied. New technologies have two exciting implications: (1) they can be used by individuals across the autism spectrum, whatever their cognitive capabilities might be; and (2) they fit in well with the current zeitgeist, meaning that in today's world, everyone uses these technologies, so that those with ASD do not stand out.

An early application of technology to help children with

ASD manage day-to-day tasks was the visual timer. A timer placed in a prominent location in the individual's daily environment helped the individual gauge how much time was available for completing certain tasks and, therefore, meeting expectations. Over time it became clear that a timer that showed time elapsing helped even more. An additional technological application was simply a watch with an alarm, which could provide a prompt to move on to the next activity. Once an older child, teenager, or adult had learned a sequence of events and the auditory cues to signal each event, the wristwatch became a way to become alert to the need to move to the next activity. These auditory cues have been shown to be very effective, as long as the person being cued is able to stay alert and respond to the cue. This kind of cue has become instrumental in helping those with ASD develop skills for independent functioning.

Cell phones can be useful for helping students with ASD, with very minimal verbal skills, contact an adult if they are confused or lost. Taylor, Hughes, Richard, Hoch, and Coello (2004) taught three students with ASD to carry a vibrating pager and an index card with pertinent contact information with them while in community settings with an adult. Once the adult separated from the teen so the adult was no longer in sight, the adult would activate the pager. At that point the teen would approach an adult in the environment, such as a store employee, and present the index card. The card conveyed information about how to reach the responsible adult and requested that the reader remain with the student until the adult found them.

Hoch, Taylor, and Rodriquez (2009) taught teenagers with ASD with verbal skills in the 3- to 4-year range to use a cell phone paired with an index card to seek help from others if they lost contact with an adult in a busy setting (grocery store, mall). In this study, the students were trained to answer their cell phone and follow the instructions to find a responsible adult, say "Excuse me," and hand over the index card, which contained the text: "I am lost. I cannot speak. My teacher is on this phone. Please speak to my teacher. I have autism." After many practice sessions (at least 10–15) in the school setting and with familiar adults, these students practiced the procedure in community settings with adults unaware of the project.

One problem with this study is that adults in the community did not always respond to the student's approach. Thus, the students were trained only to approach store employees or community officials, such as a police officer, to have the best chances of success. The investigators pointed out that although most students with autism can be taught to use a cell phone, only 28% of teens and adults with ASD have cell phones, in contrast to 89% of the typical population. Thus generalization and maintenance of the skill can be practiced regularly, since cell phone use is so widespread.

Additional devices include pagers or handheld counters (such as those used to keep score in golf). Pagers can be set ahead of time to help a child or teen remember to complete certain tasks. Angelesea, Hoch, and Taylor (2008) provided vibrating pagers to three teenage boys with ASD who would eat so quickly at meals that their behavior was socially stigmatizing. Each individual was trained to take a bite only when the pager (secreted in his pocket) vibrated, so the cue was completely unobtrusive. All three boys learned to tolerate the pager, wait for the pager to signal that they should eat something, and then stop and wait for the next signal. The pagers vibrated at varied intervals to simulate a more naturalistic approach to eating as well as to help the teens stay attuned to the pager and not merely learn the time interval. The experiment resulted in more socially acceptable eating behavior for all three teens.

Taylor and Levin (1998) worked with a 9-year-old student with an ASD who struggled to make verbal initiations to peers during play. The student was in a regular education second grade but tended to make very few spontaneous comments to adults or peers. The student was trained in 10-minute sessions, one to three times daily, after school, to make social initiations to adults, first with prompting from an adult and then through training to initiate a comment when the pager vibrated. Initially he was instructed to keep the vibrator on the desk so that he would notice when it was activated. Over time, the student kept the vibrator in his pocket and made comments to the adult when cued. The comments were initially scripted, but over time the student was able to elaborate on his verbalizations. Finally, the student was placed with other students during the school day, engaging in multiple play activities, and the student was prompted through the vibrating pager to make comments intermittently. The student's peers responded to his comments and did not seem aware that the pager was signaling his behavior. The investigators did not use prompt fading in this study, which would be the next step for this intervention.

Those with ASD may be ostracized for asking too many questions (in a classroom) or calling a friend too frequently. In our clinic at Yale, we have helped teens set up an explicit rule limiting the number of questions asked during a high school class, keeping in mind that the student with ASD needs answers but that peers become very annoyed if questions seem excessive. The teen uses their cell phone to keep a tally of how often they are asking a question or engaging in a behavior so as to abide by the guidelines previously set by the teen and the therapist. A critical piece of this intervention, however, is to help teens understand that while there are ways to get answers (in a classroom for example), they must limit their question asking in the moment.

Another innovative technology currently available is the iPrompts application, which can be used on either the iPhone or the iPad to help individuals with ASD understand the sequence of events coming up, what their choices are, what events they may be encountering, or how much time they have to engage in a particular activity. The iPrompts application allows the user to take photographs of objects or events in the immediate environment that will have significance to the person with autism, as a way to help the affected person organize and visualize upcoming events. It includes an on-screen timer as well as a visual image that shows time counting down, to help gauge how much time is left to be spent on a particular activity. This simple handheld device, with the capacity for adding dynamic photos and cues in real time, has real potential for helping parents, educators, and community providers manage their students in day-to-day life.

Video modeling, as described previously, can be very effective in teaching children how to analyze or to behave in social situations (Simpson, Langone, & Ayres, 2004). During group intervention for children with ASDs between the ages of 8 and 11 years at Yale, we used video clips from current movies and sometimes television shows to help children understand the social cues, verbal expressions, facial expressions, gestures, and body language that conveyed meaning about the social scene. It was helpful to be able to pause the video to hone in on particular cues to highlight them for the students (Koenig et al., 2010). The children were able to talk about what they thought was happening and, when they were filmed, to note changes they thought they should make in their own behavior.

Silver and Oakes (2001) used a computer-based intervention to teach children with ASD how to recognize facial expressions. The children were ages 10–12 years, with expressive vocabulary measured by the British Peabody Picture Scale of 7 years or greater. The program, called the emotion trainer, contained a series of exercises to enhance facial emotion recognition. Children were randomly divided into two groups, only one of which received the intervention. At the conclusion of training, children in the treatment group showed improved skills in facial emotion recognition.

The investigators in this study enumerated reasons why computers might be a good medium for intervention for those with autism (Silver & Oakes, 2001, p. 302), including the following:

- Focusing on a computer screen may help to screen out extraneous information.
- Computers are consistent in the way information is presented, so students do not have to cope with change as frequently as they might if a person is teaching.
- The program provides clear expectations and consistent rewards.
- The program can be geared to the child's level of cognitive functioning.

Using video games to entice children with ASD to learn new social skills has been explored by Tanaka and colleagues (2010), who have designed a set of interactive video games, titled *Let's Face It!*, that helps children learn to identify faces and facial expressions. Tanaka's program is grounded in the research on face-processing impairments in children and teens with ASDs, specifically deficits in processing the whole face versus isolated parts of the face, and lack of attention to the eyes. In a randomized clinical trial of 79 children and teens with ASD, 42 children were assigned to the video game condition and 37 children remained in a wait-list condition. After 20 hours of video game time, the children in the treatment group showed greater ability to recognize faces based on holistic features, which is the strategy employed by typically developing children. The investigators did not examine how these improvements might impact social functioning in general, but as a step toward building a foundational skill, it is an impressive use of technology.

The next level of technology is Bluetooth. Satriele, Nepo, Genter, and Glickman (2007) developed strategies using Bluetooth open wireless technology to help teens with ASDs with limited language capacity function in community settings. Once again it is important to remember that social functioning is not limited to recreational activities but is crucial for day-to-day functioning, making purchases, taking the bus, riding an elevator, or going to a museum. In this study, the investigators taught teens with very limited language skills to make a purchase at a store by using Bluetooth technology. The student learned to enter a store, select an item for purchase, take it to the register, slide his debit card through the machine, and complete the purchase, all with guidance from an interventionist not present in the store. This provided the student with a set of prompts for completing a task in a community setting without the need for an adult prompter by his side.

Gerhardt (2009) used Bluetooth technology to teach a young adult with ASD, with limited language and social skills, to take a city bus to and from work on a regular basis. The individual was acclimated to the Bluetooth technology and taught to respond to communication from his therapist. The therapist and student practiced taking the bus many times, with the therapist gradually decreasing proximity to the student. Following repeated training, the student was able to travel on the bus independently, staying connected to his therapist via technology if needed.

New technology innovations for use with students with ASDs are virtual environments and avatar-based computer applications to teach recognition of social cues and social situations. The data on these kinds of intervention is scant, but some research is beginning to explore the possibilities (Bolte, Golan, Goodwin, & Zwaigenbaum, 2010; Orvalho, Miranda, & Sousa, 2009; Trepanier et al., 2008).

Using technology-based instruction has a host of possibilities for helping students with ASDs learn new skills, including social skills, with new applications being developed every day. The challenge is not to let our fascination with the technology itself get in the way of thoughtful planning about the child's particular skill set and impairments in social functioning.

Case Example

Maria is a 13-year-old eighth grade student of above average intelligence who is mainstreamed at her local middle school. Maria is on the periphery of a social group; she has some acquaintances to sit with at lunch but is minimally engaged in conversation, and when she does speak, her topics are odd and do not lend themselves to further conversation. She focuses on her own topics and does not ask questions, offer supportive comments, or engage with others about their concerns. Her peers are not overtly mean to Maria, nor do they seek her out for social contact, in school and after school. Maria's team realizes that most girls of Maria's age have cell phones and spend time texting back and forth, even when they are in the same room. In an effort to help Maria get involved in the social scene in an age-appropriate way, her team decides that having her parents get her a cell phone and teaching her to text might make her a more acceptable social partner to her peers. Maria's parents agree, and the school resource room teacher works to teach Maria how to use the phone and texting functions. Maria catches on pretty quickly to this, and her next task is to get contact information from other girls she would like to connect with. Maria starts by asking every teen at her lunch table to provide their contact information, and they do, during one lunch period. Some eyebrows are raised among the other kids, who are wondering why she is seeking their contact information.

Once Maria has done this, she begins texting the other kids, saying hello, asking what's up, or telling them something she is doing. She gets some initial replies, to which she responds immediately, and she continues to text those who have replied and others, at a rapid rate. Over time, replies drop off, and soon few peers are responding to Maria. Also, responses to her invitations to get together have not been successful.

In this example, helping Maria learn to use a cell phone and text others was a great idea for getting Maria involved with other kids in an age-appropriate way. The problem was that Maria's basic impairments in conversational skills—including listening and responding to others and providing opening comments that ask for a reply—were not in place. Further, some courtesy relevant to texting, such as not excessively texting any one person, needed to be taught as well. For this intervention to work, Maria might have been taught to text her resource room teacher, parent, or sibling until she had the mechanics down correctly, could manage the etiquette of texting, and learned explicitly what to say and what not to say (topic choice and maintenance). She might also need to learn some of the abbreviations used in texting, and then practice with one peer (recruited by the school team) who has agreed to not only text back and forth but also give her feedback about inappropriate comments or use of the phone. In this example, Maria must learn the rules for social interaction for her age group as they are tailored to texting.

GROUP SOCIAL SKILLS INSTRUCTION

Widespread in the community, in schools, and in clinic settings are groups for children with ASDs, some including typical peers and some not, most often described as social skills groups (Bellini & Peters, 2008). Some schools call these groups "lunch bunch" because they are modeled as social practice experiences that occur during lunch and include a student with an ASD and typical peers. What happens in these groups varies widely. Some groups follow a commercially published curriculum or treatment manual (Koenig et al., 2010; Tse, Strulovich, Tagalakis, Meng, & Fombonne, 2007; Yang, Schaller, Huang, & Tsai, 2003); some include various activities designed to help children learn discrete behavioral skills such as turn taking in conversation or making eye contact (Barnhill, Tapscott Cook, Tebbenkamp, & Smith-Myles, 2002; Barry et al., 2003). Other groups use a loose set of activities with few clear objectives or ways to measure a child's progress in social competency. The research literature does not provide strong support for this approach as a general means for promoting social competency at present, although some studies showed positive effects related to helping children develop specific behaviors. Generalization of skills learned in group settings has not been well studied.

Ozonoff and Miller (1995) worked with a group of high-functioning adolescents diagnosed with ASD to promote their ability to take the perspective of another. While these students improved on specific measures of perspective taking as a part of the study, they showed no improvement on social skills on a valid, reliable questionnaire. Webb, Miller, Pierce, Strawser, and Jones (2004) described significant improvement in four of five behaviors taught in a structured intervention, but again, no concomitant improvement in social skills broadly measured. In a study with elementary schoolchildren with ASDs, Solomon, Goodlin-Jones, and Anders (2004) taught a wide variety of social skills, some of which showed improvement (face recognition skills) and some did not (perspective-taking skills). Following a 12-week, broad-based social skill program for children with pervasive developmental disorders, which included practice negotiating with others, children showed improvement in social communication but no significant improvement in social awareness (Tse et al., 2007).

Koenig et al. (2010) implemented a 16-week group program, using direct teaching, role-play, practice, reinforcement, and peer tutoring to teach social interaction skills to children ages 8 to 11 years. Parents reported improved social behavior at group's end during an interview, but a parent-completed standard questionnaire showed limited improvement.

Whether improvement is measured by direct observation or by interviewing the child, parent, or teacher, the reports tend to be inconsistent. However, this may reflect the fact that the social behavior of children with ASD in these groups may change depending on the setting or the child's degree of familiarity with various others.

Despite these varying outcomes, successful strategies implemented in group settings included a cognitive-behavioral approach (Bauminger, 2007; Chung et al., 2007; Cotugno, 2009; Morrison, Kamps, Garcia, & Parker, 2001), structured methods for teaching and reinforcement (Ozonoff & Miller, 1995), video modeling, role-play, and practice (Kroeger, Schultz, & Newsom, 2007; Morrison et al., 2001; Nikopoulos & Keenan, 2003; Ozonoff & Miller, 1995). It is clear that some evidence-based methods, implemented in a group setting, can be effective. Whether there is a specific benefit to implementing these interventions with other children in a group setting is less clear. Nevertheless, it seems likely that group intervention using peer tutors (an evidence-based intervention) and implementing evidence-based strategies, such as video modeling, is likely to be helpful.

The most significant concern with respect to the effectiveness of group intervention is whether skills taught and practiced in a group will generalize to other settings and with other people. Unfortunately, most of the research on group intervention has not carried out more extended study of maintenance over time and generalization to new settings. It seems clear that without practice of newly learned skills in carefully planned, structured opportunities outside of the initial practice environment, it is not likely that skills will generalize. This latter point is critical when evaluating the efficacy of social skills groups in community or school settings.

That said, there is data on what aspects of group intervention may show positive results. For example, an intervention group is most likely to be successful when the following components are included:

- Group members are screened to consider whether other psychiatric challenges might interfere with learning; if present, those children are excluded for the present.
- Group members include a mix of children with different levels of social and communication impairment.
- Group members attend regularly, the group meets at least weekly, and the length of the group is at least 16 weeks, with a longer interval, perhaps 24 weeks up to a full academic year being preferable; group membership is consistent—dropping in and out is not allowed.
- Peer tutors are selected to participate, based on their interest and willingness to commit to participation for the entire program.
- Peer tutors are trained using descriptive and explanatory information (see peer mediated approaches) regarding the children with ASD, their needs, and the behavioral responses toward the children expected from them.
- The group is structured in terms of scheduled activities to provide predictability.
- The group activities are geared toward developing particular skills and informal play time in which children are encour-

aged to practice new skills in the context of real-life activities.

• Activities are planned to help children generalize skills to new settings.

Case Example

Kathy and Debbie decide to begin a social skills group in a clinic for children with ASD. All children are 8 and 9 years old, three boys and two girls. Two peer tutors are recruited, who are 10 years of age. Each child is screened individually to ascertain that the child does not engage in any challenging behavior that could pose a danger to group members. Stereotypic behavior is not a reason for exclusion, since this behavior may hinder a child's acceptance into a social group, and as such will be a target for intervention. Once the children are selected, parents are presented with written materials that describe the logistics of the group, the expectation that each child will attend every week, and that parents will intermittently meet with the group leaders to discuss the child's progress. Parents highlight one or two behaviors they see as obstacles to social success for their child. Parents are told that if the child displays aggressive behavior or uncontrollable outbursts, they may need to remove the child from the group for that session. Thus, parents need to stay in the building during group.

Once the group members have been chosen, the peer tutors spend two 1-hour sessions learning about ASD (pitched to their level of understanding as 10-year-old children) and learning a little bit about each child entering the group including that child's strengths and vulnerabilities. The children are also provided with a set of guidelines as reminders of how they may interact with the children in the group (Figure 5-1).

Each group begins with greetings, an outline of basic behavioral rules, and an introduction or review of the reinforcement system (e.g., whether it's receiving stars or poker chips to be traded for prizes), once again depending on what is meaningful to the children in the group. Leaders introduce the schedule, which is depicted using text and pictures, in a prominent place in the room. Typically, the schedule includes a structured learning activity embedded in a game, a snack, free conversation and play, and wrap up. In this group, the leaders do not have the children complete worksheets, nor do they expect the children to engage in extended discussion about why it is important to make friends or to behave in particular ways. These topics are covered, but they are learned through *activity* and *coaching,* not discussion. The intervention is individualized for each child, and it happens during play.

During the first few weeks of the group, the leaders identify behaviors that each child needs to modify to improve social functioning, based on their observations and parent report. Leaders select one or two behavioral objectives for each child, once again considering the child's learning profile and what behaviors cause the most problems. Kathy and Debbie construct a worksheet to provide information about each child, and identify two target behaviors to address (Figure 5-2).

Obviously the children do not all share the same issues, but they can work consistently on changing behaviors and improving social skills in a group context. The leaders not only identify the behaviors that are problematic but also consider what the source of each behavior might be. Behavior is communication—behavior has meaning, so to help the children modify their behavior, the group leaders need to assess what function each behavior serves. For example, does Anna mumble because she lacks confidence that anyone is interested in what she has to say? Why is she so disheveled; does she get support at home for dressing? Is she able to monitor where her body is in space as she moves around the room? Does Leo pace and use scripted phrases to block out interactions from others, or does he want to interact but not know what to say? Is pacing

	Behavior	Initial Objectives	Strategies
Anna	Disheveled in appearance; mumbles when speaking; scripts from video and television.	1. Improve personal appearance. 2. Speak clearly and with greater volume; reduce scripting.	Group members delevop signals to cue Anna when she needs to adjust her appearance. Group members help Anna practice speaking more clearly, perhaps using TV talk show game.
Leo	Makes noncontingent remarks; scripts from TV/video; stereotypic rocking and pacing; can't sit for more than a minute without moving.	1. Reduce constant movement. 2. Reduce scripting and noncontingent remarks.	Group leaders identify a reinforcement system for Leo to reduce noncontingent remarks that involve the whole group, as well as a cueing system for reducing movement.
Callie	Constantly dominating the group discussion, talks loudly, screams if others interrupt; loses temper if she loses a game; critical of others.	1. Improve frustration tolerance. 2. Reduce critical comments and excessive talk.	Board games are selected in which there are no winners such as the Ungame or Mountaineering. These are chosen to help her enjoy without becoming anxious about winning. All coach and praise Callie for positive comments about others.
Oliver	Talks over others regarding reptiles and species of birds; brings all conversations back to these topics; brags about his intellect; comes to group with food on his face.	1. Reduce special interest talk/talk about his intellect. 2. Improve personal appearance and eating habits.	Group talks with Oliver about his interest in reptiles for a predetermined length of time. At each group, Oliver's talk time is reduced by 5 minutes; the group leaders encourage him to talk fast to bring humor to the exercise. After about five groups, he has less than a minute and he works with a peer to find new topics.
Ari	Speaks softly and in monotone; mostly scripted (but appropriate phrases), often is not attending to group games or social chat during snack; makes no effort to participate.	1. Attend to group members/ activities. 2. Develop more elaborate conversational scripts.	Peer tutor and one group leader sit on either side of Ari, redirecting him to the activity, and prompting him to take a turn or answer a question. Leaders devise a game in which Oliver and Callie tutor Carlos and Ari on how to converse with others.

Figure 5-2. Initial plan for group intervention.

his way of handling his anxiety? What makes Callie so sensitive about losing a game? Does she feel ignored if not the center of attention at all times? Why does Oliver talk incessantly about reptiles and fall back on the topic at every turn, even when told that others are not interested? Does he realize this behavior is alienating to others? Why is Ari spacing out during every group? Does he have any motivation to connect with others, or is he going through the motions because his parents are insisting he come to group? Without some hypotheses about the answers to these questions, the group leaders are unlikely to plan effective strategies.

For the purposes of this example, however, the group leaders proceed to outline some strategies to begin the intervention process (Figure 5-2). These strategies will change over time as the group members get to know each other, and the leaders learn more about why the children behave as they do. In this particular group intervention, based on Koenig et al.'s (2010) model, the challenges each child faces are made public within the group in a sensitive and gentle way over time, and children are encouraged to help each other learn new strategies and replacement behavior.

Additionally, each peer tutor is given a single instruction prior to the group, and the group leader makes sure to reinforce the tutor when the tutor intervenes. For example, in this group, a peer tutor might be instructed to "sit near Ari, greet him, and redirect him if he seems to not be attending; occasionally make a comment to him." This might be the single instruction for this tutor for several weeks, until Ari gets comfortable and begins to respond. If he does not respond or actively resists, the group leaders will need to create a new strategy for helping Ari with this challenge. The objective here is to help Ari get comfortable with the new behavior of staying engaged with the group. Prompting and reinforcement can be used, of course, but there should be ongoing observation of his behavior to determine why it changes when it does, and what is reasonable to expect.

For each child in the group, the leaders develop simple strategies to address each objective and then develop more sophisticated strategies as time goes on. Of course, strategies change when they don't work! Planning for each group involves a fun and possibly silly activity, in which children are coached to practice their target skills, in the context of a game. Members are complimented on their strengths and encouraged to help their friends work on their objectives. As an example, to help Leo reduce remarks unrelated to the topic at hand, a system is set up so that if he makes an appropriate remark, he gets a blue poker chip, and if he says something off topic, he gets a red one. The chips are placed in a clear plastic jar so everyone can see how things are going. If Leo has more blues than reds at the end of the session, everyone in the group gets a reward (a Tootsie Roll, a popsicle, or whatever the kids might want to work for). The group leaders encourage everyone to help Leo, making it a fun activity, and Leo starts to work for the group's approval and reward. In our groups at Yale, we found that even the most socially disinterested child could be engaged in this kind of game.

The leaders should be documenting the progress of each child on objectives, using a simple tally of behaviors for each group if that works, and graphing a child's progress over time. This helps the leaders see what activities lead to successful interactions and which fall flat, as well as what level of reinforcement and practice is needed for each child. In addition, children and parents can be taught strategies that help with targeted behaviors, and both can keep a log of how effective the child is in implementing new behavior and curbing undesirable behavior in naturalistic settings. Prompts, reinforcement, and self-monitoring strategies must be customized for different settings. In Figure 5-3, we show improvement in Callie's

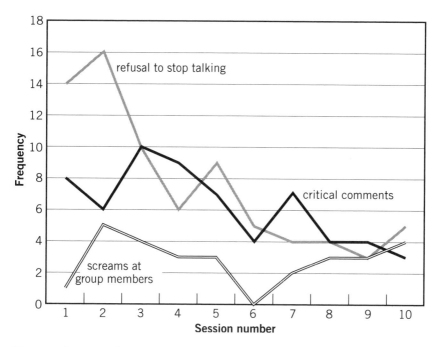

Figure 5-3. Graphing progress.

behavior, but of course, in many situations we would see much more variability, indicating that we need to make changes in what we do.

After a period of perhaps 6 months in a group intervention, an assessment of functional social behavior, using the PDD-BI or VABS (Chapter 2), would be helpful for measuring progress.

DEVELOPING SELF-REGULATION AND
SELF-MONITORING STRATEGIES

A significant proportion of children and adolescents with ASD have difficulty regulating their emotions and behavior. These challenges are often rooted in impairments in communication,

both in understanding language and nonverbal communication and in being able to communicate their thoughts and
emotions. Of course, the earlier the intervention related to
communication impairment takes place, the less likely that
children will experience behavior problems that endanger
themselves, their family, or their peers. As described previously, once children display challenging and aggressive behavior in a social setting, the more likely it is that peers will avoid
interaction.

As children learn adaptive methods to express their distress and make changes in their situation, these methods of
self-regulation become internalized and help the child cope
with challenging situations across settings and people. The
better young children learn to communicate information such
as, "I don't know," "I need a break," "I'm confused," or "Would
you repeat that question?" the better able they are to interact
effectively with the adults in their life. These are very simple
strategies that can be taught to children of any age to help
them self-regulate. Further, for children who cannot verbal-
ize these statements, signing or visual cueing can be very helpful.

A more broad-based strategy focused on helping children
with ASD take hold of their present, and possibly challenging,
experiences is to concretize their past experience through the
use of an explicit narrative strategy. Developing narratives for
an individual child is a bit like helping a child develop visual
and text-based chapters about his life and experiences that
then come together to help him construct an ongoing narrative about himself. Repeated experience reviewing these narratives helps the child develop a foundation for who he is and
where he fits in terms of family, school, and community. This
kind of cognitive grounding helps a child have a way to compare and contrast new experiences and make social decisions
based on what he understands. Typically developing children

are easily able to take in, encode, remember, and relate memories to new experiences as a way to help them interpret what is happening in any particular situation. As described in detail in Chapter 1, children with ASD experience great difficulty remembering and sequencing their experiences to form a coherent narrative. This difficulty is significant because it impacts how children and teens interpret their current experience. A detailed description of how narratives can be developed is included at the end of this section.

Hume, Loftin, and Lantz (2009) stated that challenges for developing independent functioning in those with ASD are related to the core deficits of the impairment (social and communication) as well as challenges with organization, planning, and generalization of skills to new settings. These investigators noted that the consequences of poor independent functioning are poor long-term outcomes in terms of housing, employment, and developing relationships. In turn, over 50% of individuals studied in a broad-based analysis had outcomes considered to be poor or very poor (Hume et al., 2009). Part of the problem is that, up until graduation from high school, which is often at age 21, these students spend large amounts of time with a paraprofessional who may not be trained to help the student decrease dependence on the available adults. A focus on promoting initiation skills, increasing generalization skills, and reducing prompt dependence has not been systematically included in their educational programming (Hume et al., 2009). Once these students leave what must be a fairly sheltered setting, they are at a loss as to how to organize their day-to-day lives, as well as how to focus on a realistic future.

Sticher et al. (2010) designed a program focused on helping students with ASD from ages 11 to 14 years improve basic social skills as well as self-monitoring and self-regulation skills. They taught specific curricula regarding emotion recognition, theory of mind skills, and executive functioning skills to promote the use of metacognitive strategies, that is, self-monitoring (observing oneself) and modifying behavior to adapt to social circumstances. In other words, these children learned how to specifically check themselves to see if their presentation and behavior was consistent with their peers and the current social setting.

During group intervention at the Yale Child Study Center, we have used a simple bead counter or other visual support to help younger children monitor particular behaviors we wanted to see increase or decrease. In one group we used the bead counter to help a child keep track of how many times he diverted the conversation to his special interest. While a group leader began using the counter over the course of several groups, we gradually transferred responsibility for counting to the leader and the child, and then ultimately to the child. His peers were encouraged to keep him honest about his recordings. A reward was provided at the end of the group if he had limited his remarks about his special (and unusual) area of interest. Most important was that over the course of the 16-week group, the child grasped the idea that talking about his special interest was not always welcomed by peers or adults.

A critical aspect of self-monitoring and self-regulation is establishing whether children with an ASD are able to recognize and monitor their own actions in contrast to those of others. While some investigators have speculated that this is more difficult for children with ASD than typically developing children, recent investigations have not confirmed this hypothesis. Williams and Happé (2009) examined the ability of two groups of children with ASD to monitor their own actions in contrast to the actions of others and found no differences between the groups. Children with ASD were well able to recognize their own agency, whether it pertained to actions they performed while playing a game or when playing the role of another individual playing the game. The investigators noted that the children in the experimental condition were all able to engage in verbal commentary as they played the games, and they wondered if this commentary helped to scaffold the child's memory and understanding of the sequence of events. In this regard, support for using visual or textual narratives would help children to self-monitor. Although not part of the experiment, the investigators wondered if children with more compromised verbal and cognitive skills would have done as well.

As noted in Chapter 1, narration to complete a task is best exemplified by very young children who talk themselves through a task or rule as they complete some action. It is not uncommon to hear preschoolers or other young children repeat out loud, or softly to themselves, what they intend to do or what they are expected to do. For children with ASDs, developing a personal history based on a repertoire of past experiences is helped by creating narratives with text and visuals. This provides an internal template on which to base new experiences. Essentially, the process is this:

- Choose an activity to document as a narrative; it may be helpful to choose something entertaining and fun as a way to help your child understand this teaching and learning experience.
- Take digital photographs of the child as he or she proceeds through the experience, from dressing, to getting in the car, arriving at the event (zoo, beach, picnic), going through some of the activities at the event, wrapping up the day, getting in the car, and heading home.
- Use PowerPoint or a word-processing program to create a book for the child, or use Snapfish or iPhoto to put the pictures together in sequence with very simple text.
- Read and review the book with the child so he or she remembers the sequence and can answer simple questions about the experience.

- Use the book to elaborate on experiences, in a very simple way.
- Help the child refer to the book to review his or her experience, and relate it to other activities.

For a child with limited language, poor narrative skills, and very poor ability to conceptualize his life experiences as a whole, this kind of exercise will go a long way toward helping with self-conceptualization and self-regulation. Experiences that don't go well because of unexpected circumstances or upsetting events can be chronicled as a way to make events seem less catastrophic and to problem solve other ways to manage changes or upsets. While typically developing children build an internal history of their experiences and their reactions and the ways they coped with challenges, children with ASD may need an explicit set of visual and textual supports to accomplish the same thing.

COGNITIVE-BEHAVIORAL TREATMENT

Cognitive-behavioral treatment (CBT) is an intervention in which a therapist works with an individual to help change behavior by addressing persistent thoughts and feelings that lead to nonadaptive behavior. CBT has a strong evidence base for effecting change in children, adolescents, and adults with anxiety, depression, and behavioral disorders. More recently, the conceptual underpinnings of CBT have been based on helping individuals to identify "retrievable memories of adaptive responses that can successfully compete with and suppress memories of previously learned maladaptive conditions" (Wood, Fujii, & Reno, 2011, p. 198). Further, discussion with the affected individual and "Socratic questioning" are used to help the individual think about responses to prior situations, thoughts and feelings during those situations, and how the individual might develop new skills to change behavior in the future. A handful of studies conducted with children and adolescents with ASDs have demonstrated that CBT can be effective in treating comorbid psychiatric disorders such as anxiety or depressed mood (Chalfant, Rapee, & Carrol, 2007; Reaven et al., 2009; Sukhodolsky et al., 2008). For example, Sofronoff, Attwood, Hinton, and Levin (2007) demonstrated that children with Asperger's disorder as well as disruptive behavior improved their anger management skills following CBT.

White et al. (2010) developed a treatment manual targeting anxiety and social impairment in children with ASD, recognizing that in higher-functioning individuals, recognition of the lack of social connections and loneliness may lead to anxiety and depression (see Bauminger & Kasari, 2000). The investigators developed the Multimodal Anxiety and Social Skills Intervention, which is based on principles of CBT. Rather than using the Socratic method for exploring issues described earlier, the manualized curriculum is didactic in nature, which is more likely to be comprehended by those with ASD. This curriculum includes principles of ABA, since strategies based on ABA have a strong track record for effecting behavior change in those with ASD. Further, modeling, receiving feedback from peers, using visual supports, using drama, and using cues are included as well. In this way, this program adapts CBT to the specific learning profile of children and teens with ASD. What is also impressive about this program is that it includes individual treatment, group treatment, and parental involvement. A pilot study of four young teens with ASD showed that the program was feasible to implement and acceptable to the teens and their parents. Families were compliant with the recommendations of the program (White et al., 2010).

In terms of implementing a CBT program with an individual with ASD, it is important to remember that the term *high-functioning* can be very misleading. A student with an average or above average IQ score may have no ability to integrate social information whatsoever, and an extremely limited ability to construct a narrative reflecting what has happened in the past or what is happening in her day-to-day experience (see Chapter 1). Organizational thinking skills and planning skills may be weak, and thus CBT conducted in sessions may have little impact on the child's functioning in day-to-day social situations (Koenig & Levine, 2011; Ventola, Levine, Tirrell, & Tsatsanis, 2010).

Case Example

Margaret is a 17-year-old diagnosed with ASD. She is mainstreamed in high school and attends all classes appropriate for a high school junior, although she is tracked into the core classes (versus college-bound classes). Margaret's cognitive profile ranges from average (nonverbal problem solving) to low average (verbal problem solving) skills. Her current placement in core classes is a result of below-average adaptive functioning skills, including immature socialization skills, inconsistent hygiene practices, and very poor coping when frustrated (screaming episodes, but no physical violence).

Margaret's team knows that she needs to be working on transition planning, because she hopes to attend a community college, which is well within her purview with regard to her academic performance. The team worries about her adaptive behavior in the community college setting. The school psychologist decides to set up weekly individual sessions with Margaret of 40 minutes in length to target adaptive skills. While the psychologist is clearly the interventionist here, she sets the tone for the meetings as one of collaboration and preparation for independent living. Margaret and the school psychologist identify together, over a period of time, the behaviors Margaret needs to modify to be successful in college. This is done gradually, sensitively, and in a very collaborative way, so Margaret feels that she is the author of both the list of concerns and the primary author of the solutions to these issues (although she can acknowledge support when needed).

Discussions of the topics, issues, and other students that provoke Margaret's temper in class are developed with visual strategies and diagrams to help her visualize the events that upset her, and similarly, develop specific strategies for coping (such as taking a break from the classroom). In some cases, the topic that provoked the upset must be deconstructed in detail before focusing on what we would consider an appropriate response. Given the challenges that children and teens with ASD have with overfocus on details without grasping the gestalt, Margaret may need to explain how she understood a situation, how she reacted, and why, before she can tackle the issue of her screaming behavior (Koenig & Levine, 2011).

Other issues, such as those related to hygiene, are discussed as a set of rules to be followed, and magazines geared toward teenage girls are used for the teaching tools (not textbooks). Every week or two, Margaret and her therapist set goals for improving hygiene, and a system of self-monitoring is set up, so that Margaret becomes the one to document whether she has followed through. Since ultimately this particular set of issues comes down to Margaret's investment and willingness to follow through, it is not particularly helpful to get parents highly involved.

In this scenario, the psychologist (supported by the team) has developed a cognitive-behavioral model for helping Margaret build social skills (including hygiene and coping skills) through one-to-one therapy sessions. There has been no involvement of peers for modeling purposes, nor guided practice of skills in alternative settings to probe for generalization. While the therapeutic relationship between Margaret and her therapist is a source of support for Margaret, and she is improving inconsistently with regard to hygiene and coping in the classroom, the wraparound structure (involvement of peers and interventionists in multiple settings) and practice that works well with those with ASD is not in place. It is not clear whether Margaret will be able to learn and maintain these new skills on her own.

In summary, the evidence for CBT for social impairment in children and adolescents with ASDs is limited. Skills that are characteristically impaired in ASD such as perspective taking, abstract thinking, adept verbal skills, constructing meaningful narratives about past events, and planning ahead seem to be requisites for effective CBT. If treatment can be modified to address these issues, as has been done with White et al.'s (2010) model for anxiety, future treatment may be successful.

PARENT-DELIVERED INTERVENTION

Parents are members of the child's intervention team and, as such, need to be involved in decision making and intervention at different points along the way. The enormous challenge this poses for parents and team members cannot be overestimated, and more in-depth information regarding how parents and providers can work well together is described in Chapter 6.

This section focuses on approaches to intervention that are taught to parents who use the approach or strategy to work directly with their child to improve the child's social functioning. The research in this area is limited, but there is a very strong push of late to develop evidence-based interventions that can be disseminated more broadly in community settings—that is, beyond the school environment (Interagency Autism Coordinating Committee, 2011). Here I have reviewed a few of the leading studies in this area but certainly have not covered them all.

The most focused efforts to date have been on helping very young children with ASD develop social reciprocity skills (Aldred, Green, & Adams, 2004; Aldred, Pollard, & Adams, 2001; Gillett & LeBlanc, 2007; Kasari, Gulsrud, Wong, Kwon, & Locke, 2010; Schertz & Odom, 2007; Smith, Buch, & Evslin Gamby, 2000). Smith, Buch, and Evslin Gamby (2000) developed a parent-directed, intensive intervention based on principles of ABA. Six boys diagnosed with ASD, 35–45 months of age, participated in a treatment program in which their parents and other interventionists (family members or college students) were trained to deliver the intervention. Parents and therapists attended 36 hours of training on how to teach the children how to respond to requests, converse with others, and make friends with peers. The format was one-to-one sessions (similar to a discrete trial format), but once children mastered some basic interactive routines, sessions were conducted in a group setting, such as a classroom with typical peers. The efficacy of the intervention was tested after 5 months, and follow-up was conducted between 2 and 3 years later. The investigators found that five of the six children made important gains in the first 5 months of treatment, particularly with regard to verbal and nonverbal imitation and correct responding to directives. At the 2- to 3-year follow-up point, two children showed gains, while others showed little change, and one child's IQ and adaptive behavior scores were lower than the baseline score. The investigators speculated that quality of implementation of the intervention—as it was administered—influenced outcome, but since they were not able to measure this directly, it could not be confirmed. Further, while some parents may have continued the intervention following the 5-month intensive intervention, there was no information about how frequently or how intensively this might have been done. A final speculation regarding the inconsistency in outcome was that the easiest skills to teach and learn were addressed and mastered in the first 5 months and more sophisticated interaction skills, such as making and keeping friends, were harder to teach.

Aldred and colleagues (2001, 2004) developed a program for teaching parents how to understand the foundational skills that lie beneath competent communication and social interaction. Their intervention began with a series of parent workshops on many topics, for example, one in which parents learn how to deal with their own feelings related to communication breakdown with their child and how this can be repaired. Once parents are trained in a series of techniques to engage their child, videos of parent-child interactions are used to help parents understand how best to interact with their child to promote (1) joint attention skills; (2) synchronous interaction; (3) predictable structure for the child to establish a foundation for enlarging interaction in the future; (4) variation in interaction and communicative teasers (similar to the communication temptations used in Pivotal Response Treatments or SCERTS intervention; and (5) modeling appropriate language.

This model acknowledged the challenges that parents feel when their attempts to communicate are not successful and what kinds of responses may occur (Aldred et al., 2001, 2004). Some parents give up and communicate less and less frequently to their child, while others develop a controlling style of interaction with the child. While this response is completely understandable, the outcome is that children become less likely to initiate communication, and parent initiations become more rigid and directive.

In a quasi-experimental study, 14 children with ASD, median age 48 months, were treated and compared with 12 children with ASD in a treatment-as-usual condition. Aldred et al. (2004) found that parents trained to adapt their communication styles to their children, with reduced controlling and intrusive responses, showed improvements on reciprocal communication scores on the Autism Diagnostic Observation Schedule and on measures of parent-child interaction. Interestingly, there was no improvement on measures of parent stress, suggesting that there is more work to be done to help parents feel more effective with their children and at the same time more relaxed.

Some studies focused on teaching parents how to intervene targeting early foundational skills, particularly joint attention (Kasari et al., 2010; Schertz & Odom, 2007). A small study of three toddlers and their parents showed that two of the three toddlers developed joint attention skills, and the third toddler, while not reaching this milestone, developed improved skill at focusing on faces and participating jointly in activities with others (Schertz & Odom, 2007). This intervention assisted parents in thinking through what kinds of preferred activities would be easiest to work with in terms of engaging their kids. Parents were exposed to a specialized curriculum for promoting joint attention skills, which helped them devise appropriate activities for their children; however, the specific activities were not prescribed. In this intervention, what is important is the degree to which the parents were encouraged to use knowledge of their children and the children's preferences to develop intervention, rather than being taught to implement strategies that may or may not fit into the interactional style of their family and community.

At present, the most comprehensive and rigorous study of parent or caregiver training to promote foundational skills in toddlers with ASD was conducted by Kasari et al. (2010). This randomized controlled trial of 38 caregivers of toddlers with ASD included 19 children-caregiver pairs in active intervention and 19 children-caregiver pairs in the wait-list condition. As a baseline measure of parent-child interaction, a 15 minute videotape was filmed to assess the pair's ability to either (1) be jointly engaged, (2) show the child's interaction with an object, or (3) show no engagement between child and caregiver. Raters blinded to the condition of the child-caregiver pair, in terms of treatment or wait-list, rated the interactions based on

15 minute videotaped interaction. The investigators further measured the caregivers' self-report about their adherence to the treatment, which included coaching the caregiver-child pair in play routines, working on imitation and simple conversation about what the child was doing, expanding on the child's communications, and making environmental adjustments (e.g., seating) to help the child stay focused on the interaction.

The results of this randomized controlled trial showed no differences in primary scores on engagement, joint attention, or play at baseline, but that following intervention, children in the active treatment group engaged in less object-related play and participated more in joint engagement activities. In a 1-year follow-up, these gains were maintained.

The significance of this level of improvement in foundational skills, that is, those needed for communication, cannot be understated. This clinical trial showed that caregivers, properly trained, could implement an intervention with high fidelity to procedure that would help their children move from object-related play (non-interactive engagement) to engaged interaction. Investigators found that the quality of "buy-in" to the intervention by caregivers predicted improved outcomes, and recommended greater study of these issues (Kasari et al., 2010). In a very crucial way, this study raises more questions than it answers and suggests that intensive follow-up is needed for a multiplicity of questions. Clearly, the advantages of training parents and other caregivers must be exploited, given the prevalence of ASD to date.

Too often, the contributions of master clinicians are not considered when examining the effectiveness of intervention to promote skill development in children with ASD. The work of Aspy and Grossman (2008), Baker (2003), Bellini (2008), Coucouvanis (2005), Loomis (2008), Quill (2000), and Sussman (1999) are excellent examples of how knowledge, expertise, and experience come together to provide insights into effective intervention for kids with ASD. In the realm of translating intervention approaches from professionals to parents, a number of expert clinicians have taken the lead. For example, Baker (2003) recommended thoughtful planning by parents prior to arranging any kind of social interaction between a child with an ASD and a typically developing child. Further, Baker recommended that parents work with a child to set up rules and practice skills needed to be successful in a play encounter, including playing with the other child rather than playing in parallel. Additional lessons include working with the child with ASD to teach compromise, taking turns, and coping with losing a game.

The Hanen Early Language Program, published in 1999, is a comprehensive curriculum designed for parents to support early communication skills in children with ASDs (Sussman, 1999). This volume focuses on practical strategies, with an empirical basis, that will help parents understand their child's communicative attempts and foster ongoing communication and growth. The initial volume by the Hanen Group, titled *More Than Words*, provides explicit instructions to help parents learn to understand their child's communication (no matter how idiosyncratic), follow the child's leads (within reason), help the child take turns and make connections between people and communications, help the child use visual supports, and learn from books and toys. *More Than Words* is one of the most user-friendly books for parents, breaking down concepts that seem complex into basic elements that any parent can understand, and providing many examples for how parents can implement strategies to promote communication in their child.

An important contribution to the literature on promoting social development in children with ASD for parents comes from Dr. Jim Loomis (2008), author of *Staying in the Game:*

Providing Social Opportunities for Children and Adolescents With Autism Spectrum Disorders. Dr. Loomis's book focuses, as would be expected, on helping children develop interactive social skills, but the most critical aspect of his work is helping parents understand how and when to help their children fit into and manage social activities happening with typically developing kids. Loomis describes how parents can assess social opportunities for their child to consider if the fit is right, how to work with their children to provide the right amount of support (not too much and not too little) to get them involved in a social scene, and how to use peer mentors and adult facilitators. Essentially, the objective is to help children with ASD and their peers have fun together, seek out further opportunities to explore relationships and experiences, and discriminate between those who will accept differences in social presentation in a child with ASD and those who are not secure enough to do so (with the imperative not to engage with those individuals).

Less extensively studied are strategies using parents or caregivers to promote social interaction and increased social competency in teenagers with ASD. This may not be surprising since, in developmental terms, it is not typical for parents to be involved in arranging social opportunities for their teenage children. At the same time, children with ASD, despite chronological ages of 13 years and above, may be delayed with respect to emotional and social maturity up to 5 or 6 years, so that their social needs are at a very basic level, perhaps closer to those of a child of 8 or 9 years of age. If this is the case, it is reasonable to assume that these children have not mastered the social and emotional tasks of prepubescent children (8- and 9-year-olds). There is every reason to believe that helping them master these social and emotional tasks (see Chapter 1) will help them develop competent interpersonal relationship skills as opposed to pushing them forward to a level (age 13 or

14 years) where they are unlikely to comprehend the social interaction or manage it effectively.

In an attempt to address these complex issues, Laugeson, Frankel, Mogil, and Dillon (2009) developed a parent-assisted social skills training program to improve friendships in teens with ASDs. The investigators expanded their model of friendship training, based on extensive work helping children with ADHD and fetal alcohol syndrome, to children with ASDs. They targeted skills such as developing conversational ability, developing friendship networks, handling teasing and bullying, practicing good sportsmanship, and practicing good host behaviors when entertaining others. A central focus of this program was developing "peer etiquette," defined as the evidence-based rules of behavior enforced by a peer group (p. 597). In this trial, 33 teens with ASD and their parents participated. The subjects were assessed using the Kaufman Brief Intelligence Test (Kaufman & Kaufman, 2005) and the Vineland Adaptive Behavior Scales, second edition (Sparrow et al., 2005). The investigators used parent and self-report measures to determine improvement in social skills following a 12-week course. Parents participated in educational sessions on how they might help teens expand their extracurricular socialization network, how parents could come to understand the teen socialization scene and where their child might fit, and how parents could supervise teen get-togethers and help teens plan such events. Results indicated that teens in the treatment group learned more about relationships (based on their answers on a paper-and-pencil test), and that those teens also initiated more social gatherings than those in the wait-list condition. There was no increase in the number of invitations for socializing from others in the treatment group as compared with the wait-list group. The investigators speculated that the failure of the teens in treatment to receive new invitations might be because the treatment was brief, and this may have not been enough time to build and cultivate relationships.

As a whole, the most successful parent-directed interventions are those that have helped parents understand and promote development of the foundational skills needed for authentic social connections. As with many of the approaches in this book, the essence of promoting social development begins with ensuring that the child has the opportunity to learn social competence skills (as described in Chapter 1), rather than learning discrete social behaviors only. Education of parents with regard to these issues becomes an important role for school and community providers. In fact, IDEA 2004 mandates parent counseling and education, which includes "providing parents with information about child development and helping parents develop the necessary skills that will allow them to support the implementation of their child's IEP" (Wright & Wright, 2007, p. 201).

SOCIAL STORIES

Social Stories is a technique for intervention developed by Carol Gray (2000), an educational consultant to the public school system in Jenison, Michigan. A social story is aimed at increasing a student's understanding of a situation or skill by helping the student attend to relevant contextual cues as well as prescribing how the student ought to behave in that situation. Gray explains that social stories provide a product for the affected individual. This means that the story conveys respect for the student's perspective and helps all parties to understand the issues that are the focus of the story. Considering that children with ASD have trouble thinking in the moment about how to behave when upset or confused, and that they may have strong rote memory skills and an affinity for rule-based situations, this technique seemed promising. Initially, the stories were used to help children with challenging behavior anticipate upsetting situations and follow explicit guidelines for behavior at those times. Also, these stories focused on very basic skills such as learning to chew gum quietly, listen to school announcements, set the table, wash hands, use the shower, play with a dog, or ask a question in class. Gray and Garand (1993) published a description of several students whose behavior improved when they were read social stories prior to encountering problematic situations. They argued that these stories were effective teaching tools because they provided students with information that they would not typically attend to in an everyday situation. They posited that this technique would be helpful in reducing behavioral problems, teaching academics, and helping with social problems.

Gray and Garrand laid out general principles for constructing social stories:

- Writing the story from the perspective of the target child.
- Keeping the story short (perhaps four to six sentences at most).
- Using descriptive sentences to delineate the problem situation.
- Using perspective sentences to describe how others might be thinking or feeling about the problem.
- Using directive sentences to help the student know how to behave.

Later, two additional kinds of information were added:

- Control sentences, which use an analogy to explain a situation.
- Cooperative sentences, describing who might be able to help the student in a confusing situation.

Gray recommended that each story contain up to two directive sentences for every three to five descriptive or perspective sentences. The directives focused on what the child should do versus what the child should not do. The procedure was that the story was constructed and then read to the student on a regular basis, often just before the event depicted in the story was to take place. Story writers were cautioned to keep in mind the level of cognitive functioning and receptive language of the student, as stories pitched at too high a level were bound to be unsuccessful. Following a reading of the story by the student or the adult, the adult asked the student a series of comprehension questions to assess how well the child understood the story, and clarify any questions that arose. Proponents of the social stories technique argued that the technique was successful in part because students benefited from using visual cues or text and because these students tended to have excellent rote memories.

While Gray's initial study showed a positive result (Gray & Garand, 1993), subsequent research and meta-analysis (analysis of the results of multiple studies) have provided limited support for the use of social stories in effecting change in students with ASDs (Ferraioli & Harris, 2011; Kokina & Kern, 2010). Some investigators speculated that greater success is achieved when teaching single, straightforward behaviors, such as lining up in school, or reducing tantrums during homework (Chan & O'Reilly, 2008; Kokina & Kern, 2010). Crozier and Tincani (2007) noted that with regard to facilitating social interaction and communication, the child's level of motivation to engage socially is a variable that must be considered; that is, a child may understand the behavioral expectations of the story but have little motivation to follow through. In this situation, the interventionist would need to include other strategies to motivate the child to follow the story guidelines.

To date, more than 40 studies have been conducted, once

again showing weak positive effects of the intervention (Ko-kina & Kern, 2010). In part these results arise because some studies used social stories in combination with teacher or peer prompting. Other studies did not adhere to the rule regarding the ratio of descriptive and perspective statements to directive statements. Further, some studies moved away from teaching simple, concrete skills such as lining up in the classroom or putting a coat away in a cubby to more complex social skills such as initiating conversation and responding to a greeting. Given these modifications, it is hard to know exactly what is working. It is possible that this technique is more effective for concrete skills versus more complex social skills.

At present, there is not strong data to support the use of so-cial stories alone to help children learn more than the simplest forms of appropriate social behavior, such as greeting a friend or saying goodbye. This may be because the kind of prescrip-tion for behavior included in social stories does not take into account the fluid, fast-moving pace of social interaction, and the need for individuals to think quickly and respond to the par-ticular context. Nevertheless, it is possible that this intervention can be helpful with teaching basic social skills if it is:

- Used to describe and explain concrete tasks and situations.
- Used with children who need behavioral guidance in these situations.
- Used with children with ASDs who have a Verbal Compre-hension Index of 68 or higher on the Wechsler Intelligence Scale for Children, fourth edition (based on research by Quirmbach, Lincoln, Feinbert-Gizzo, Ingersoll, & Andrews, 2009).

Case Example

Andrew is a 12-year-old boy with autism, borderline intellec-tual skills, and receptive and expressive language in the borderline range as well. He was slated to begin a group intervention to promote social skills at a local hospital clinic, near the same location in which he had been evaluated by psychiatry, psychology, neurology, and genetics specialists. Andrew tended to be fearful about coming to the clinic because previously he had blood drawn on two occasions, and he would typically escalate his behavior, screaming and hitting his mother, when they drove to and walked into the clinic. Despite repeated attempts to convey to Andrew that this clinic experience would not be painful, and could be fun for him, he had a hard time holding onto this information.

A simple story was constructed, supplemented by a digital photograph for each statement that described what would occur:

- On Monday afternoon my mom drives me to the clinic.
- I wait in the waiting area with my mom and the other boys in my group.
- At 3 o'clock, I go with the other boys into the group room.
- I sit on my mat and listen to the group leader.
- I play with the other boys, and then we have a snack.
- The group ends at 4:30 P.M., and I walk to the waiting room.
- My mother is waiting for me, and we go home.

This story helped Andrew understand the sequence of events and to overcome his fear of coming to the clinic on a weekly basis. He was able to read the story multiple times prior to the first few group sessions, then no longer needed it. Importantly, the story was focused on helping Andrew know what would happen and what he was to do. It did not address his previous experiences, nor did it provide detailed instruction on social interaction with others.

Overall, the strategies described in this chapter can be combined with one another or used in different settings to teach the same skill. The essential issue is that the team stays focused on why behavior occurs or does not occur, and what strategies might be best for a child. It will be different for every kid!

CHAPTER SIX

Parents and Professionals as Partners

• •

The common refrain in every text or presentation describing intervention for children with ASD is that parents and professionals must work together or the child suffers. We hear this and believe it, but making it happen is a whole different story. Poor communication or disagreement among parents and professionals makes collaboration challenging and often unsuccessful (Simpson, de Boer-Ott, & Smith-Myles, 2003; Strassmeier, 1992). Many times the conflict among the adults is discussed behind closed doors or not discussed at all. If raised in team meetings, the atmosphere may become tense and sometimes poisonous. By the time the discussion is out in the open, a due process hearing is under consideration. So how should we address these issues?

What we know is that telling everyone that they have to get along and cooperate does not have any earth-shaking impact on how people conduct their work. Perhaps parents and professionals need to step back from opinions and discussion about the child to get clear about their functioning as a team and how well each team member understands the point of view of those with whom they work (Simpson et al., 2003). A senior member of our Yale team said once that the reason she thought we were generally successful in terms of our work is that "we think with one head." By this she did not mean that we always agree about a child's learning profile, the social challenges the child faces, or the reasons why problem behaviors have arisen. Rather, what she meant is that we as a team understand each other's way of viewing children and families, our ways of approaching issues, and our professional orientation. This level of knowledge about how each professional conducts his or her practice makes collaboration easier. To function effectively, we need to know what really goes on in the heads of parents and professionals as they attempt to collaborate, sometimes successfully and sometimes not. Figure 6-1 lists the team members that might be included in the care of a child with autism.

- Representative of school administration
- Parents
- Regular education teacher
- Special education teacher
- Speech-language pathologist
- Occupational therapist
- Physical therapist
- School psychologist
- Guidance counselor
- Community professional, such as social worker, psychologist occupational therapist, or speech therapist
- Social worker
- School nurse
- Pediatrician
- Psychiatrist
- Paraprofessionals

Figure 6-1. Possible team members.

Consider the problem of Jonathan, a 7-year-old boy in the second grade who is diagnosed with an ASD. Jonathan shows high average intelligence but below-average receptive and expressive language skills. Jonathan has a tantrum whenever it is time to leave recess and return to the classroom in the afternoon. This did not occur the previous year, but since it has begun to happen, his peers are avoiding him on the playground and in the classroom. He is upset about this, as is his mother, and school days seem fraught with tension for Jonathan, his teacher, and his peers. Jonathan's teacher implements a visual schedule to help him anticipate the change in activity, so it is clear that he understands what needs to happen. After a week with no change in the frequency or duration of tantrums, Jonathan's teacher decides that a 5-minute reminder before it is time to line up might be helpful. She implements this strategy, but it seems to make things worse, as Jonathan now begins to get upset as soon as he is given the warning. When asked why he gets so upset with the instruction to line up for the restroom and to return to the class, Jonathan can only say, "I don't want to!" The playground monitor tells the teacher that Jonathan is a "spoiled kid" who "always gets his way" at home, and that Jonathan understands the expectations perfectly well. In her view, Jonathan should have an unpleasant consequence (lose recess time for the next day) if he throws a tantrum. Jonathan's teacher prefers to use positive reinforcement for desirable behavior, so she makes sure to praise Jonathan if he manages the transition better than usual. She is considering the aide's suggestion, but really feels Jonathan needs his recess time.

Next, Jonathan's teacher consults his mother, Mrs. Delito, in an attempt to clarify the situation. Mrs. Delito says that this difficulty with transitions does not happen at home. She seems to think Jonathan's teacher is not handling the situation correctly but cannot offer any suggestions on what to do differently. Now the teacher is more frustrated than ever. She manages to get Jonathan in every day, but it takes an extra 10 minutes for him to return to the classroom because he is the last child in and needs to be taken to the restroom by the playground aide, after the other children have used the restroom and returned to the classroom. The teacher praises Jonathan regularly if he manages to get himself in with only minor fussing, and she has done this from the start, even though it has not seemed to help very much. The paraprofessional is less sympathetic with Jonathan and tends to be firm and sometimes quite curt with him. The teacher can see their less-than-positive relationship deteriorating further, and she knows she will need to work with this paraprofessional, and with Jonathan, throughout the school year. Next, Jonathan's teacher works with the school social worker to write a social story to help Jonathan understand the routine. The story shows Jonathan on the playground, lining up quietly, using the restroom, and returning to class. Jonathan is happy to read the story with the social worker every day, often right before recess, and sometimes it seems to help a little bit, but not consistently. Just when the teacher is feeling at the end of her rope, she has a conversation with the music teacher, who tells her that Jonathan cannot tolerate the part of music class when children are allowed to use instruments, and typically, the cacophony sends him running into the hall. His teacher realizes that the boys' restroom the children use after recess is a huge space with loud echoes and lots of children yelling and banging doors. She writes a new story in which Jonathan goes with the classroom aide to a restroom near the classroom, which is more recently refurbished and less cavernous, 3 minutes before recess ends. Jonathan is able to follow this routine well, and no further issues arise.

In this example, what begins as a behavioral problem for Jonathan and school staff quickly turns into a social problem.

Children who show challenging behavior at school are at risk of peer rejection, and once a child has established a reputation among peers, it can be very difficult to turn things around. Further, Jonathan's relationship with his teacher and the playground aide seemed to be at risk, as well as his mother's relationship with the teacher, and perhaps the school. In this situation, Jon's teacher tried many strategies with some evidence of efficacy (using a visual schedule, cueing, social stories), so she clearly had some knowledge about what might work. Communication with Jon's mother was a potentially good step, but communication with the music teacher was what ultimately helped to solve the problem. Thus the need to know the child well, to know what approaches and strategies might help, to test multiple strategies, and to work with the whole team to plan intervention are highlighted.

The other important issue to be highlighted here is the professionalism and strenuous efforts of Jonathan's teacher. Fortunately, she solved the problem, although it took some detective work to get it right. This kind of scenario happens all the time in school settings, and fortunately, teachers who have a firm knowledge of ASDs would most likely reach the same conclusions that Jonathan's teacher did. The danger, however, is when school staff or parents get frustrated with each other, the child suffers, and the situation deteriorates.

A second concern is that team members might conclude that "visual schedules don't work with him," "social stories aren't helpful," "Jonathan doesn't do well with a 5-minute warning; there's no point in trying this strategy again." It may be the case that certain strategies *are* better than others for Jonathan, but this problem was solved through team effort, through understanding the source of Jonathan's behavior. Having access to a professional with expertise in functional behavior assessment would have helped the teacher as well.

When we approach a problem with a child with an ASD,

164

we consider the child's personality and the context as important information for understanding why the child thinks and behaves as he or she does. Actually, the same information about team members is needed to understand the dynamics of the team working with a child with ASD. Let's focus for a minute on the adults surrounding the child.

In an ideal world, parents and professionals would put aside their attitudes, beliefs, prejudices, fatigue, and mental stress to collaborate effectively. Since we do not live in that ideal world, it turns out that parents and professionals are beset by a host of pressures that influence the way they think about their work and how they function day to day. Much has been written about the stress and coping styles of parents who have a child with ASD (Bailey, 2010; Boyd, 2002; Hastings, 2010; Koegel et al., 1992; Kuhn & Carter, 2006) but less about how professionals handle the stress of working with these children (Jennings & Greenberg, 2009; Ransford, Greenberg, Domitrovich, Small, & Jacobson, 2009; Strassmeier, 1992; Williams, Johnson, & Sukhodolsky, 2005). In this chapter, the stresses and strains for both sides are summarized, providing background to inform discussion of collaboration.

THE EXPERIENCE OF THE PROFESSIONAL

Professionals working with children with ASDs may include, but are not limited to, regular education teachers, special education teachers, speech-language pathologists, paraprofessionals, occupational therapists, physical therapists, psychologists, pediatricians, psychiatrists, school guidance counselors, social workers, and special education administrators. Of course, each professional brings a certain amount of knowledge and experience to the table. Beyond that, a host of factors are in play as people go through their day, some helpful and some not so helpful.

As of 2008, school professionals were expected to do more work with fewer resources and supports than ever before (Ransford et al., 2009). The average teacher, who worked 37.7 hours weekly during the school year 2003–2004, is now working about 50 hours weekly (Ransford et al., 2009). In the current climate, there is an unprecedented expectation that school professionals take responsibility for the emotional and social growth of their students (Individuals With Disabilities Education Act, 2004; No Child Left Behind, 2001; Ransford et al., 2009). Those who entered teaching expecting to help students learn and be excited about specific content and ideas find their role expanded to teaching social and emotional skills. Teachers and other school personnel have commented that they were not taught how to address these issues—and so feel less than qualified (Jennings & Greenberg, 2009).

The focus on yearly testing in school districts throughout the United States adds additional pressure, since teachers are under great scrutiny by school administrators, who are, in turn, pressured by the state to achieve particular scores on the statewide exams. No Child Left Behind (2001) includes sanctions for schools that are not performing, incurring further costs to school districts. States are faced with the penalty of stretching their already limited funding for poor performance—not exactly a positive behavior support approach for change! Ransford and colleagues (2009) concluded that since a student's performance is determined by a variety of factors outside of the teacher's control, the pressure for student performance creates extreme stress. The expectation to produce results when a teacher does not have control over all the factors that influence those results is truly untenable.

In general, regular education teachers feel poorly prepared to address the needs of students with ASD (Simpson et al., 2003). Without formal knowledge regarding the disability or guidelines for designing inclusion programs, these teachers become overwhelmed and lose confidence in their ability to do their job. Simpson and colleagues (2003) stressed that these teachers (and other members of the child's team) need accessible ongoing collaboration with others and available support service staff (such as paraprofessionals) as well. All available research confirms that workshops or time-limited in-service training programs are not effective in providing the kind of team support and consultation needed to program for these students (Ransford et al., 2009; Simpson et al., 2003)—ongoing consultation is what is required. An additional critical element of successful program planning for students with ASD is support from administrators (principals, special education directors, superintendents). Finally, school personnel must deal with family reactions and responses to the child and how the child's disability impacts the family.

Burnout refers to a situation in which school personnel feel overwhelmed, ineffective, emotionally and physically exhausted, and sometimes cynical about the impact they can have on students. Strassmeier (1992) studied the stress level of teachers and other professionals working with special needs students and found that many of the special education teachers reported chronic exhaustion, an inability to relax, and a feeling of inefficacy with respect to their work. Causes of burnout can include limited support from school administration, conflicts with colleagues regarding approaches to students, feeling inadequate to meet the learning needs of students, time and paperwork pressures that seem unending, poor compensation for hours spent, and pressure from school administration and parents to do the impossible. Pertinent for our discussion is that a significant source of burnout is inconsistent cooperation between teachers, lack of discussion about the content and methods of teaching, and problems that arise with regard to how school personnel, in the heirarchy from administrators on down, relate to one another in general (Strassmeier, 1992).

In a study reported in 2009, teachers were evaluated on their ability to implement a social-emotional curriculum for kindergarten through fifth grade (Ransford et al., 2009). The investigators measured the teachers' attitudes about teaching the curriculum as well as their psychological experiences. There were strong associations between how well and how frequently teachers implemented supplemental instructional material from the social-emotional learning curriculum, and how well they generalized and integrated the lessons during other parts of the school day. Teachers with the highest levels of burnout showed the poorest implementation of the curriculum.

Are these facts any surprise to a professional reading this material? Doubtful. What is a surprise is that these facts are sometimes ignored when school teams meet to plan intervention for children with special needs. The best administrators know this information well and find a way to support their staff, but in some cases, the idea conveyed to school professionals is that they need to keep their personal feelings and professional opinions under wraps, in order to present a united front to parents in a team meeting.

It is worthwhile to consider the configuration of a team constructed to work with a child with ASD in the school setting, and also to consider the impact of an external consultant, whether a psychologist, educational consultant, or pediatrician. In this situation, school personnel may welcome the input of the community professional or feel threatened by that person and her input. They may have had experiences with that particular consultant prior to this situation in which they felt criticized, unappreciated, or not validated for their hard work. It would be great if the school professional could put this kind of history aside, but it is naive to think it could happen easily. The consultant may have similar ideas about members of the school team, again, which are hard to put aside.

Another issue is that school professionals differ in training and in orientation. One behaviorist with a firm orientation toward behavioral principles may view a child's behavior as a form of escape while another behaviorist with a more developmental approach may integrate behavioral principles with an understanding of the child's current developmental stage—in contrast to chronological age. A speech-language pathologist may view certain behaviors as clear communications about the child's state of mind, emotional experiences, and needs; and finally, an occupational therapist may see the child's behaviors as related to sensory needs. As professionals, it is the responsibility of each individual to consider other points of view and to respect those whose training and experience has led them to different conclusions about the child's challenges and behavior. If this is not happening, the school administrator or team leader must address the conflicts within the team directly and actively resolve them. To side with one team member over another breaks down trust and morale and leads to disjointed intervention and little likelihood that the team will be able to work together effectively in the future. It is startling to hear of situations in which team members attempt to quash disagreements during a team meeting with the misguided notion that this kind of behavior will fool parents and will not impede the child's progress. Before we consider what might be done to improve these conditions, let's consider the experience of parents.

THE PARENTING EXPERIENCE

Parents of a child diagnosed with an ASD go through numerous emotional and social stages related to their child's growth and development that profoundly impact their own state of mind. Additionally, these parents, like all parents, have baggage to carry in the form of expectations based on prior experiences, extended family expectations, community expectations, and their own needs. Most parents of a newborn have notions of the nearly perfect child, the child who will have all the academic, musical, athletic, and social talents they did not have; maybe a child who will redeem them in eyes of others (whomever they might imagine others to be). When reality hits and it becomes clear that every new baby has a unique personality, with strengths and vulnerabilities related to genetics and constitution, this can be a blow to parents with high expectations. This is no less true for parents of a child who develops an ASD than parents of a typically developing child. Imagine the grief and distress of this parent, who hoped for a particular child with unique talents and skills, only to find that the child seems less able to cope with the day-to-day world than most other children his or her age. Beyond this, parents report experiencing fresh waves of overwhelming grief when their child makes a transition (perhaps to camp or a new school) when they see typically developing children maturing rapidly.

The process of early assessment for ASD can be arduous. Bailey (2008) describes that parents come to initial meetings regarding their child with a mix of feelings, perhaps wanting to know if something is wrong and at the same time not wanting to know, and not always trusting the professionals assessing the child. If the child has been previously diagnosed, parents may have positive impressions of the professionals that participated in the assessment or not, and these impressions carry over to future interactions. The pressure on parents is unrelenting, and there is the looming worry, no matter what the age of the child, about the permanence of the condition and what it means for the life of the child and the family (Boyd, 2002; Koegel et al., 1992).

At the same time, parents can feel supported at the time of diagnosis, with resources available to help them learn what the diagnosis means, what help is available, and how the community (early intervention, school district) can provide support. Sometimes parents ask for predictions about their child, but of course these are impossible to provide. In many ways, it is frustrating for parents to hear this, but it is important to try to refocus them on short-term goals, and to help them prioritize (Bailey, 2008).

Mothers and fathers of children diagnosed with an ASD are at increased risk for mental health problems, such as depression and anxiety (Hastings, 2003, 2010). When strategizing with parents regarding an intervention approach to be implemented at school and at home, professionals may not be aware that a parent may suffer from insomnia, poor attention and concentration, chronic anxiety, depressed mood, irritability, hopelessness, helplessness, feelings of worthlessness, and low energy. Mothers and fathers may have feelings, sometimes unexpressed, of guilt and personal failure, as if they have done something wrong that has increased the likelihood that the child developed an ASD. Unfortunately, extended family members may reinforce this mistaken belief. Rogers and Dawson (2010) pointed out that cultural expectations play a role in how parents perceive their child's disability and how the extended family may perceive it as well. Raising typically developing children is challenging enough, so imagine the strain on a parent with additional pressures and symptoms trying to implement special strategies at home. Stressed parents are less likely to be effective when interacting with their children than parents that are not feeling stressed (Hastings & Beck, 2004). Children who have severe behavioral problems can raise stress levels significantly, since parents are often afraid to take them out in public. Children with sleep problems can be irritable and tired throughout the day, and parents of children with sleep problems are often sleep-deprived.

Families cope in a myriad of ways with the stress and strain of having a child with an ASD. Following a diagnosis, parents may adopt rigid roles for coping (Bailey, 2008). Sometimes, but not always, fathers throw themselves into working to earn what is needed to cover extra services and supports, while mothers take on more day-to-day management of the child. The marriage may become strained and the child's siblings may feel left out of the family in some ways, because of the focus on the affected child. Sometimes both parents avoid dealing with the child as much as possible if the child offers little social reinforcement or is behaviorally difficult to manage. This can lead to guilt and feelings of failure as a parent, which increase the likelihood of mental health problems and relationship problems.

A large body of research literature has found that mothers of children with ASDs experience higher levels of stress than mothers of children with other developmental disabilities (Hastings, 2010; Koegel et al., 1992). Mothers of younger children may feel more stressed than those of older children. Mothers of children with ASDs express feelings of inadequacy and low self-efficacy, which are clearly demoralizing. Dr. Kyle Pruett, clinical professor of child psychiatry at the Yale Child Study Center, speculated that mothers feel particularly demoralized when coping with a child with no or low social motivation to interact because, traditionally, mothers take on the role of helping children develop social and empathy skills, although, of course, fathers contribute as well. Dealing with a child who does not naturally show social connection, empathy, and engagement might be particularly demoralizing to a mother who sees these qualities as important to impart to her children. Unintentionally, parents may interact less with their child because of the minimal feedback they receive (Koegel, Koegel, Vernon, et al., 2010), further slowing the process of building communication skills. Slow and inconsistent progress can be discouraging, and the constant worry about whether a better treatment might be available somewhere else makes parenting exceedingly hard (Rogers & Dawson, 2010).

These issues become more difficult because parents often have to deal with a cadre of professionals to obtain services for their child. This requires excellent organizational and communication skills, which some parents may not have. The more parents feel that they are effective in helping their child, the more likely they are to feel less anxious and depressed (Kuhn & Carter, 2006).

KEEPING THE FOCUS ON THE CHILD

Actually, there are ways that teams made up of parents, school professionals, and community professionals can work together to craft an effective intervention plan for a child with an ASD. Essentially, it depends on whether the team can agree on areas in need of intervention and can communicate with each other regarding their views about why these areas are problematic and what possibilities exist for remediation. In the beginning, team members do not need to agree on why behaviors or areas of need exist, only that they do exist. Each team member should consider how the behavior manifests and hypothesize about the source of the problem, considering that the behavior or lack of appropriate behavior may have more than one function even if the form of the behavior looks the same (Powers, 2005). Compiling detailed descriptions of a particular problem (e.g., a child repeating scripted phrases at inappropriate times and places) and how the problem shows itself in different settings (e.g., home, school cafeteria, classroom, playground) will help the team dissect the problem so that relevant information can be gained about what internal or external events trigger the behavior. During this discussion, it is helpful to remind everyone that children with ASDs are quite prone to behaving very differently in different situations (that's the norm). Further, the degree to which different observers agree on what a child is doing or not doing is very low; agreement is typically about 20% (De Los Reyes & Kazdin, 2005). This is not because some observers are better at understanding or observing than others, but rather because all the observers are right. When parents say that a child "never does that at home," it is likely true, and the next step is to find out why. If the team can discern why disparities are occurring and then isolate the variables in the environment that make something work in one environment and not in another, it is a step in the right direction. Essentially the team has to use the informant discrepancies to explore the behavioral data to identify functions of behavior, and in turn design intervention to address behavior (De Los Reyes & Kazdin, 2005). Too often, teams get caught up in disagreement about how severe, how frequent, or how problematic a behavior is, and cannot get past this. The disagreement festers, and the team is not able to move forward productively. At such times it is hard to remember that everyone—professionals and parents—is working hard to understand the child and the behavior in the service of helping the child to learn.

IT CANNOT BE LEGISLATED: TRUST

No one can deny the advantages of the federal laws that have provided equal access to a free, appropriate education for students with disabilities, including students with ASD. Further, the groundbreaking work by so many scientists, educators, and clinicians—too many to mention—has far advanced the field in learning how to make sure these children learn, develop, and grow up to lead productive lives. We have to acknowledge that the vast majority of those in the fields of education, special education, or community services for children with ASD are not in it for the money. The truth is that educators, parents, and clinicians are motivated by the desire to see children be educated and productive to the best of their ability. Sometimes, it is hard to believe that, but it's true.

An experienced, talented, and extraordinarily successful special education teacher working with elementary school students described what she believed to be the key element that makes the difference between a functioning, effective team and a struggling team: "It's all about trust." When families and professionals trust that there is honesty, openness, and a genuine desire to work with the child to address developmental and social concerns, the process of the child's education moves forward smoothly. When there is distrust, suspicion, hard feelings, or the belief that somebody on the team doesn't get it, the team flounders, and so does the child. When schools and families engage in contentious communication, the child suffers. It's the sad truth, but it is the reality. Essentially, working to understand the team as well as the child makes all the difference.

PROMOTING COLLABORATION

Collaboration begins when team members drop their defenses about their work and their opinions and strive toward authentic communication with each other. School administrators have a huge and incredibly daunting task, because their job is to address the needs of the students and families, while taking good care of their staff and managing their budget. As parents and professional staff, we may rage about the financial issues that play into how services are disbursed in any particular system, but this is the reality.

Within the team working with a particular child, not only does each person have a formal role, but there are informal roles as well. One particularly vocal team member with a strong personality may have the power to change the direction of the discussion, for better or worse. Another team member may be talented and creative with children but less likely to participate actively in team meetings. Team members experiencing burnout may contribute to an atmosphere of hopelessness or noncooperation. Given these issues, one member of the team should be designated as the leader and have the authority to direct the meeting. The team leader needs support from the school administrator to perform in this role, and particularly to insist on respect and understanding between team members.

While it may be hard to do, the administrator or team leader must address or confront team members who seem to be hampering the collaborative process (for whatever reason). This should not be in a public setting, but there should be a frank but supportive discussion of the problem, with both individuals working toward practical solutions.

ADDRESSING COLLABORATION WITH PARENTS

A similar issue arises when working with parents. As described previously, parents come to the table with all sorts of thoughts and feelings about their child, what the child needs, and the collaborative process. Just as school or community professionals have different personal styles, parents do as well. Parents vary in their approach. Some can be passive or even emotionally removed from the process; others are collaborative in a positive way. Some parents are not able to organize themselves effectively to follow through on team recommendations, even if they want to. Parents with prior conflicts with school personnel may approach the meeting in a defensive or combative way. These issues have to be addressed as well but need a slightly different approach. A community professional working with the child and parents is probably in the best position

to discuss the parents' thoughts and feelings and how their behavior comes across in interactions with school team members. Often, parents feel safer discussing worries or concerns
about the child or the team with someone who is not on the
school team. A sophisticated consultant or community professional will work to bring about a collaborative process, rather
than allowing any conflict or distrust to escalate.

If the school team feels the need to address issues involving
parents that seem to be hindering effective collaboration, one
member may attempt discussion with the parents about it.
Since schools are not in the business of providing personal
counseling to parents, this kind of discussion must be handled
very delicately. The social worker or psychologist on the team
may be in the best position to address collaboration issues. If
the parent has a strong relationship with one professional on
the team, that person may be the best choice. This process
should not happen without express planning with school administration. IDEA 2004 requires that schools provide parent
counseling and training, which means assisting in understanding the special needs of their child, and helping them develop
the skills needed to work with their child (Wright & Wright,
2007). It does not in any way suggest that schools may use this
service to address parent-professional conflicts, and there may
be legal consequences if school professionals attempt this.
Once again, any discussion with parents about their positions
and behavior during meetings or interactions with school personnel should be cleared by the school administration.

Essentially, the success of any intervention plan for a child
with an ASD rides as much on smooth collaboration between
all team members as it does on effectively implementing evidence-based interventions tailored to the child's particular
needs.

CHAPTER SEVEN

Generalization: Adapting and Maintaining New Behaviors

• •

Our ultimate aim as we promote social development in children with ASD is to help them reach a point where they can fluidly integrate a new social behavior into their personal behavioral repertoire. What this means is that the child begins to own the new behavior, modifying it as needed based on context and over time. Without easy integration of the social behavior at the right time and place, the most well-executed behavior can seem artificial or inappropriate. This is more likely to be the case with sophisticated, higher-level social behaviors than with simple discrete behaviors.

As an example, a child with ASD may learn to say hello to friends and teachers at school but not do so when he runs across the child or teacher in a supermarket. Why? Because the skill has been taught at school, in the classroom, at the beginning of the day when the child is taking off his coat and putting his lunchbox away. He has learned that saying hello is a part of this morning routine, and he does it well. This child has learned the behavior and he performs it based on its relationship to the setting, the people, and the other particulars of that moment. He has not grasped that the purpose of saying hello is to acknowledge someone in a positive way at first sight—this is pretty abstract for a child with ASD. The child has learned the concrete skill but it has not generalized in the way that we would like. The conditions in the supermarket are not similar enough to the morning classroom routine for him to respond correctly.

In this chapter, the process of generalization is described straightforwardly, and the procedures for teaching it are described. For simplicity's sake, we use the word *generalization* to refer to extending behavior to new settings, people, and situations and to helping the child maintain the behavior over time (known as temporal generalization).

Unfortunately, few intervention studies provide information about generalization efforts, and, if they do, reports of maintenance of behavior usually go no further than about 6 months (Bregman, Zager, & Gerdtz, 2005). Also, much of the research on how to teach children to extend their newly learned behavior to new settings has focused on concrete tasks, such as learning new words or behavioral routines. This is because the construct of generalization comes from the literature of applied behavioral analysis, and so current principles guiding generalization are consistent with that theoretical orientation. The challenge here—the social complication—is that using the principles of generalization for a concrete task is much easier than using these same principles to change behavior in a social learning situation. The social situation is more fluid and contextually based, and the behavioral responses must be equally fluid. We start with generalization of concrete behavioral skills and then move on to generalization of social skills.

BASIC PRINCIPLES

Generalization means that a behavior is taught so that it is broadly conceptualized and executed by the individual in multiple settings, in contrast to understanding and executing the behavior in a single setting, in which it has been taught (Powers, 2005). Figure 7-1 depicts the basic stimulus-response-reinforcement sequence. Further, it is worthwhile to learn some of the terms used by behavior analysts, since these terms, however foreign they may seem, really do describe what we need to understand about generalizing behavior. Let's start with three terms: stimulus generalization, stimulus discrimination, and response generalization. It will be helpful to refer back to Figure 7-1 as you read through these next sections.

Stimulus Generalization

Stimulus generalization means that a particular behavior becomes more likely in the presence of a new stimulus, if that new stimulus shows features similar to a familiar stimulus to which the child has responded and been positively reinforced. As a concrete example, if a child has learned to ask for a cookie at home when he sees the dessert plate, and he is given a cookie when he asks appropriately, he may ask for an edible treat in another setting where he sees desserts available, guessing that he will be reinforced with the treat. He has generalized the initial stimulus (cookies) to desserts, and he generalizes his behavior based on the new but similar stimulus. In the example described previously, the child has failed to generalize (Figure 7-2). If the child sees his teacher in the supermarket and greets her because he expects a smile in return (the reinforcement), he has generalized the stimulus (his teacher) to a new situation. Typically developing children and adults do this all the time. They transfer a behavior based on a cue to a new situation, if the cue is the same or similar to what they have experienced before.

A child with ASD is less likely to be able to abstract the most salient information from the stimulus in order to appre-

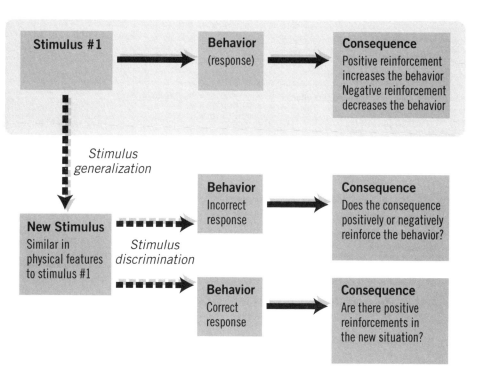

Figure 7-1. Stimulus generalization and stimulus discrimination.

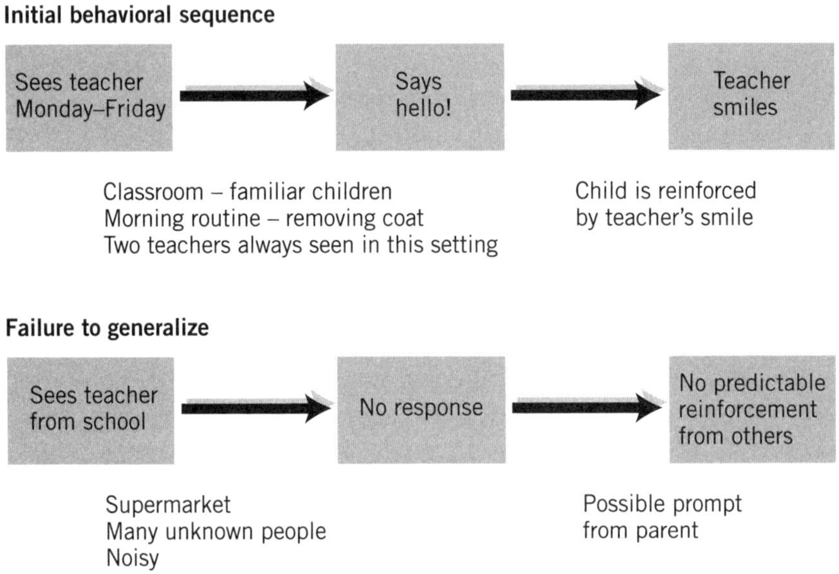

Initial behavioral sequence

Sees teacher Monday–Friday	→	Says hello!	→	Teacher smiles

Classroom – familiar children
Morning routine – removing coat
Two teachers always seen in this setting

Child is reinforced
by teacher's smile

Failure to generalize

Sees teacher from school	→	No response	→	No predictable reinforcement from others

Supermarket
Many unknown people
Noisy

Possible prompt
from parent

Figure 7-2. Failure to generalize or discriminate.

ciate that other similar stimuli require the same response (Ghezzi & Bishop, 2008). Further, other variables that increase or decrease the likelihood of generalization to a new person, place, or time may not be consistent (Powers, 2005). Finally, the stimulus that triggers the desired behavior may include other factors that we as interventionists have not counted on (Peterson, 2009).

Let's take these three problems separately. With regard to abstracting information, a child with ASD usually views situations very concretely and does not make the leap to a more conceptual understanding without help. Thus, when we are teaching a new behavior, such as a greeting, we need to make the purpose explicit to the child and then offer many, many exemplars. The interventionists might review a number of common and then not-so-common scenarios to the child, and provide opportunities for practice. Initially, the stimulus for greeting another might be augmented by a prompt from an adult, but then the child must recognize the stimulus without prompting and respond appropriately. This is where a self-management strategy might come in handy, in which the child is taught to ask himself a series of questions about the situation to determine what to do. For greeting, the child might be taught to ask himself, "Do I know this person?" If not, then he could ask, "Do the people I am with [mom, teacher] know this person?" If so, saying hello is appropriate. Figuring out a self-monitoring strategy for a social behavior is not an easy task, but the objective is that it becomes more and more automatic for the child.

Powers (2005) highlighted another problem when generalization is not occurring related to setting events and organismic variables. Setting events are conditions in the environment that support correct responding to the stimulus. The configuration of the classroom, the noise level, the children and adults present, the day of the week, and the time of day are just a sample of the possible events that set the stage for the behavior to occur. These events do not cue the behavior; they are conditions within which the stimulus occurs that support correct responding. Whether the child is tired or hungry, has just recovered from an earlier tantrum, or is thrown off by a change in the schedule are organismic variables that impact whether the child will response to the stimulus. A problem with teaching generalization is that the interventionist may not realize what setting events contribute to a correct response or what organismic variables are influencing behavior. In the example above, the team may not realize that it is not only the teacher's greeting but also the classroom setting, the time of day, and the presence of other children saying hello that set the stage for the behavior to be performed. Other variables might include who is involved in an interaction and what learning history the child has had with that individual in the past.

To address these issue, the team must carefully detail the situations in which a child is performing a behavior correctly, taking into account as many possible setting events and organismic variables as they can, considering the particular child. When a behavior is not generalizing, the two situations—the training situation (in which the child is responding correctly) and the test situation (in which the child is not generalizing)— must be compared on a very detailed level (Martin & Pear, 1988). Attention to setting events, organismic variables, and similarity or lack of similarity between the original stimulus and the new stimulus presented in the test situation should be documented. In addition, detailed information regarding how and when the behavior occurs appropriately; what starts and stops it; how long it lasts; how frequently it occurs; and what it actually looks like (a physical description) are important factors to consider (Powers, 2005).

Suppose we are teaching a child with ASD to converse reciprocally with two other children during free time at school, waiting for a bus, in the lunch line, in the hallways, and in study hall. So, we have determined what kind of behavior we want to teach, but what kind of reinforcement will the child respond to? A child with strong motivation to engage socially may be reinforced by other children's responses, but what about a child with minimal social motivation? The team may need to start with concrete rewards for correct responses, with a view toward helping the child ultimately become reinforced by social interaction.

The team may teach the child how to take turns in conversation, ask questions related to the other children's interests, comment on what others are saying, and elaborate on the conversation (a higher-level skill that would require much practice). The child should have opportunities to practice, first with adults and then in a dyad. When the child does well with this, the team may plan to test out this skill in a natural setting. Noting setting events and organismic variables as well as naturally occurring stimuli in the new setting are critical before moving forward. One member of the team might coach the child to try to converse during lunch, with just a few attempts. If successful, the child and interventionist can consider what went right. If unsuccessful, they can consider what happened to hinder the process. Practicing, using rules that the child has been taught to help with judging how and when to converse, must happen regularly, in multiple settings over time. In order not to overwhelm the child, it makes sense to practice in one setting until the behavior looks good, and then gradually expand to another setting in a systematic way. This requires careful planning by the team.

The third possible problem is that the stimulus (the event presumed to trigger the child to respond) may not be the stimulus at all. We may think we know why a behavioral sequence is triggered, but we might be completely wrong. Or the stimulus may be triggering other behaviors (that we do not want to see) as well. If a child is not learning the basic behavioral sequence correctly, prior to thinking about generalization, we must consider these issues. It might be that the adult in the situation is providing positive reinforcement for an undesirable behavior unintentionally (Ghezzi & Bishop, 2008).

Stimulus Discrimination

Stimulus discrimination means that the child learns to evaluate a new stimulus (which may look or seem the same on the surface as a prior stimulus) and decide whether the new stimulus warrants the previously taught response. For very simple tasks, this might mean that the child compares the two scenarios with a specific criterion in mind that the child can use to make a decision. Using this strategy to make decisions about social behavior is much harder because the two stimuli may seem similar, but non-tangible social information may be present in one situation and not in another, and this information guides the choice of response. Making judgments and recognizing and understanding non-tangible information are significant weaknesses for these children, so we must try to make the process concrete, perhaps by giving the child guidelines for making a discrimination. A child with ASD might be invited to play by another child on the playground, a desirable activity. She recalls that when asked to play by one child, she was welcomed and enjoyed the play, but the child currently extending the invitation has teased her repeatedly during play. She needs to use this social information to make a discrimination when the stimulus (the invitation to play) presents itself.

Since children will have to make thousands of judgments over the course of their development, the team must analyze social situations and extract as many rules as possible for making discriminations. Picture prompts, peer tutors, and family members might serve as discriminative stimuli, helping the child make a decision (Powers, 2005). To the degree possible, the team should teach the child self-management steps for social decision making and help the child practice. Unfortunately, social rules change depending on a myriad of factors, and there is only so much a child may be able to process with regard to how to make these decisions. Mistakes will be made along the way. It is probably helpful to remember that typically developing children and adults make poor social judgments from time to time.

Response Generalization

Response generalization occurs when the child begins to use varying correct responses to stimuli. Initially, the child has learned a behavior in response to a stimulus, and she may respond correctly to that stimulus or to a similar stimulus (stimulus generalization), but now she needs a host of options for correct responding. The goal is to help the child generate novel responses over time. A strategy for teaching is to use a series of exemplars, in which the student and the interventionist review multiple examples of situations in which a stimulus occurs, the child has to make a judgment about how to respond, and the child has to choose what response to make. For example, in the case of Ben, who laughed when another child was crying (see Chapter 3), he needs to work with many exemplars requiring different responses, with a cue in each exemplar that helps him know how to respond when he sees a child in distress. Children without the ability to learn multiple responses because of cognitive or language limitations may need to be taught multiple rote responses. Alternatively, they may benefit from working with an adult to set up a series of nonverbal signals to guide responses.

GENERALIZING SOCIAL BEHAVIORS

So how difficult is it to teach children to generalize the new social behaviors they have learned to diverse contexts and to maintain these behaviors over time? This is a challenge because although team members might understand the process perfectly, working to teach social behaviors and integrate social information and judgment into the generalization process is a brand new endeavor for everybody. We cannot possibly teach about every possible social contingency that may occur that will change the nature of the child's response. Essentially, the generalization plan must provide a way for the child to self-manage experiences and choose responses. Additionally, everyone on the team and in the child's diverse contexts must provide opportunities to practice the behavior in various forms. In this regard, everyone has to know what the plan is and how to carry it out. The plan for generalizing a social behavior must be designed at the time the team is deciding on the strategy for teaching the behavior in the first place. This is because they will likely need to modify elements in the first teaching environment and with regard to the chosen strategy to allow generalization to happen as the intervention unfolds. Powers (2005) commented that the strategy of "train and hope [for generalization]" coined by Stokes and Barr in 1977 has long been considered completely useless. Yet this seems to be what occurs in a majority of treatment settings (Peterson, 2009). A behavior that is limited to time, place, and a specific stimulus does not have much functional value.

When incorporating generalization procedures into an intervention plan, the training conditions should vary. This means that when teaching a specific behavior, we have to consider and balance two different principles for teaching a child with an ASD. One is that the child needs consistency and predictability to learn a new behavior, with consistent prompts, consistent rewards, and a similar environment; the second principle is that the child needs to learn to respond to varied prompts, varied rewards, and a varied environment. The key is that there must be enough consistent (familiar) elements of stimulus (prompt), environment, and reinforcement (response) to induce the behavior, but these must not be exactly the same in every situation. If the elements of a situation are unchanging, the child will become fixated on the concrete aspects of the situation and respond only when every concrete aspect is in place. Varied materials, settings, and people will help with training in this regard. If the child begins by learning a response to one stimulus, but then develops similar responses to similar stimuli, he is beginning to learn to generalize. The expression "train loosely" refers to the idea that interventionists must train responses and reinforce them, with an eye toward a broader context. In other words, the interventionist must be cognizant during the earliest training opportunities of ways in which the behavior can be prompted by varying stimuli (with a common feature) and reinforced with varying rewards (again with a common feature). For this level of intervention to take place, the interventionists must know up front the kinds of situations that the child will be exposed to and the kinds of reinforcements that are preferred.

To help children develop social judgment, training responsivity to multiple cues (Koegel & Kern Koegel, 2006) is pertinent. Here, the child with ASD who may over-focus on some aspects of the stimulus or environment needs explicit instruction to take in multiple pieces of information about a situation in order to make a judgment about responding. Again, it is important to use varied teaching techniques and instructional materials and to incorporate elements of the natural environment into the training so the child can learn the behavior with a variety of setting events and other contingencies (Ghezzi & Bishop, 2008).

The principles that hold for training generalization to new settings, people, and events also hold for training over time. There are times when a child has learned a new social behavior and is generalizing it well, but over time the behavior becomes less frequent. For example, Nicole learned to chat with those at her lunchroom table in a fairly relaxed way (Chapter 5). If the configuration of kids at the table changes, or when the school play ends (a prior topic of conversation), a strategy needs to be in place to help Nicole continue to develop and strengthen the skill. She may need to learn some questions to ask the newer members of the group to begin a casual relationship, and also how to comment on new topics that have been introduced. A learned social behavior will degrade over time if setting events and reinforcements are no longer present in the environment. Perhaps one of the kids who chatted the most with Nicole (reinforced her behavior) is no longer at the table. This will have an effect, and a strategy can be put in place to help Nicole transition to conversation with new kids.

As another example, suppose an educational team is working with Marc, a 6-year-old boy in first grade. Marc is safe in his environment and when on task, he can complete academic assignments well. The problem is that Marc tends to ignore both his teachers and his peers, unless his one-to-one classroom aide redirects him to the particular person or task at hand. This works well, but Marc needs constant redirection. Without the aide, he does not participate in classroom or academic activities independently but instead prefers to draw. The team decides that a goal for Marc is to respond when addressed, for social purposes and to follow the classroom routine. Ultimately, his parents and the educational team want Marc to respond consistently when addressed, whether for social, academic, or other purposes. Ideally, Marc's responses should be consistent and robust across all settings and over time. As one might do for other kinds of skills, it makes sense to break down the task of responding into smaller steps, teach each step explicitly, and then practice each step repeatedly with appropriate reinforcement. Next, the behaviors are chained together and practiced in multiple contexts with multiple adults and peers. Finally, situations for practicing the behavior over time and contexts are explicitly planned and then practiced at periodic intervals over the next days, weeks, and months to come.

In this situation, Marc's team notes that his interest in interacting with other children is inconsistent but is strongest when they are talking with him about his drawings. He does like winning games and collecting stars on his behavior chart, which he can use to obtain new drawing materials and extra drawing time. Marc's educational team devises a plan for teaching him to listen to instructions or social initiations consistently in his learning environment—which is not just his classroom, but the school setting, broadly speaking. First, the team breaks down the desired behavior into steps:

- Attending to four vocal signals (teacher or peer): "Marc," "listen," "pay attention," "look up here."
- Orienting his body to the speaker.
- Looking at the speaker.

Beginning with the first behavior, attending to a vocal signal, Marc's team devises a strategy they think will fit the problem and Marc's preferences. The strategy begins with a game in which Marc and a small group of peers receive a small reward for looking toward the speaker when each of the four signals are given (child's name, listen, pay attention, look up here). The children play the game every day, competing to see who can respond most quickly to the vocal cue and winning rewards for doing so. The teacher ups the ante by telling the children they will play the game at various times throughout the day, and those who are attending and responding will earn rewards. It might be appropriate to set up the reward so that the children get a colored marker everytime they win—and the first child to get the complete set earns some time to draw. The games goes on for a number of weeks, with the teacher making it playful and silly, and upping the ante by cueing children at all sorts of times and places. The team makes sure that Marc stays in the game, continuing to receive rewards and staying motivated to participate. In this way, the team is reinforcing Marc's efforts to remain vigilant in case he hears his name or any vocal signal that indicates that he should attend.

Next, the team decides to have children play the game in multiple contexts during the day, extending his learning across environments. Again, the game is played at spontaneous times and multiple settings until all children, including Marc, are earning a reward for a correct response. If Marc seems to lose interest in the game, or takes longer than is desirable to respond, the game rules are changed to re-involve him and ensure his success. As he becomes adept at monitoring adults in the environment for a signal to respond and performing the behavioral response, the game is changed so that a peer provides the initial vocal cue for responding. Over the course of several months, Marc and his classmates become attuned to listening for a vocal cue bidding their attention and responding to it. Marc's team builds on this routine by then teaching children to make more elaborate responses to requests. To promote generalization of this skill, Marc's team might have to implement this game or another game emphasizing active listening to multiple settings. Actually, setting up the game in a similar way with varying rewards would help Marc and other children be successful in different settings and with different peers. The enormous challenge with this intervention is that it requires a well-defined, clear strategy, with consistency in implementation from adults throughout the school setting and the school day.

As this example shows, there is no getting around the fact that training for generalization over time, settings, people, and situations is complex and time consuming. This is likely the reason that the "train and hope" strategy has been around for so long. Nevertheless, learning new social behaviors will not lead to true social development unless this part of the intervention process is included, right from the start.

CHAPTER EIGHT

Measuring Progress

• •

Measuring progress in developing new social behaviors and ultimately social competency in children with ASD is a thorny problem for the field. It is fair to say there have been many attempts to address this issue, but the science has been slow to develop, in part due to the complexity of the construct of social competency (Koenig et al., 2009). While we have standardized measures of cognitive functioning, language functioning, and adaptive functioning—and these measures have a set of normative values derived from a population of typically developing children—with few exceptions, the field is lacking in measures of social behavior and functioning appropriate for measuring the progress of a child with ASD over time. Another issue is that social development and behavior are extraordinarily context and culture based which makes it all the more difficult to teach and measure. What is normative in one culture for a 15-year-old young woman may be entirely different from what is normative in another culture. It is more likely that a child's team can design accurate measurements for a particular child and a particular social challenge if they know some basic principles of measurement.

MEASUREMENT PRINCIPLES

Entire books have been written on how to measure behavior from the most simple to the most sophisticated, and there is no way that this section (or this chapter) can cover the detailed science that has gone into designing accurate measurement methods. At the same time, learning some basic principles will help with understanding standard measures and help to evaluate measures to design and use.

Validity

Validity means that the method you use to measure a behavior actually measures that behavior. This seems pretty obvious, but it is more complex than it seems. When designing social objectives for a child, the outcome is both abstract and not abstract. We may be able to measure how many times a child engages in reciprocal conversation with peers during recess, but it is more difficult to measure whether the child has made a friend. As described in Chapter 3, in the discussion on individual education plan (IEP) goals and objectives, does having conversations with others at recess constitute a friendship? How far can we really go in terms of measuring social development and ultimately social success?

Here is another concrete example of a measure with limited validity. Suppose a school team has taught a sixth grade girl to manage changing in the locker room before and after gym, which is very much a social skill that involves quite a few unspoken rules of behavior. Part of the teaching included keeping things in her own space, managing dirty and clean clothing, being courteous to the other girls, not commenting on the other girls' clothes or their bodies, taking turns at the sink, and using a changing room (if that's the norm) but doing it rapidly enough to allow other students time to change. The child has had a bit of trouble in these areas, which has irritated other students, and the guidance counselor is trying to rectify this problem. Additionally, this child is spending about 25 minutes changing after gym, when the time allotted is 10 minutes so that students can get to the next class. The guidance counselor decides to check on how well the student is doing by checking her backpack before and after gym to make sure everything is there and timing how long it takes her to get through the changing process. The measurements are done every other day, and the child seems to be performing very well, with all needed items in the backpack before gym and (mostly) after gym, and a changing time that has improved from 25 minutes to 15 minutes. These are reasonable measurements as far as they go, but the measurement method does not encompass all the features of the social behaviors that have been taught. We could argue that being courteous to the other girls, taking turns at the sink, and keeping her materials in her personal space are more important socially than the timing issue. The measure is valid as far as it goes, but it does not accurately assess what we want it to measure, that is, whether the child is meeting the social objectives that really matter for getting through gym class, that is, performing in a way that is acceptable to peers.

Reliability

Reliability refers to how well the measurement we are using assesses the behavior in a consistent way. This means that when we use the measure at different times, it discriminates behavior in the same way. One way to increase reliability in a school setting or at home would be to make sure that everyone using the measure is in agreement on how to use it and how to score it. If we are measuring how many times a 5-year-old child behaves aggressively toward his schoolmates, everyone on the team has to agree on what constitutes an aggressive act.

Is it only hitting and pinching, or would it include occasional pushing in line or getting too close to another child? Sometimes it seems like this, too, is obvious, but if the measure reflects wildly different rates of aggressive acts, we have to be clear that everyone using the measure agrees concretely about what it means. It may be that the measure is in fact quite reliable, but the child's behavior is varying based on other factors. In any case, it is worthwhile to consider all the possibilities.

The other issue to consider is what we expect of children as we measure their behavior on a daily basis. We can all think of times when we forget something, let something go, or make some other kind of trivial mistake. Sometimes parents and school teams are hoping for 100% performance of a particular skill, without considering that this is unrealistic.

MEASUREMENT TOOLS FOR ASD

Some excellent rating scales and observational measures have been developed to measure social behavior in children with ASD at a single point in time, for diagnostic purposes, but whether they are appropriate for measuring incremental, subtle improvement related to response to treatment is unknown. Researchers have been experimenting with using two instruments, designed to make discriminations regarding diagnosis, to measure outcome related to intervention: the Social Responsiveness Scale (Constantino & Gruber, 2005) and the Autism Diagnostic Observation Schedule (Lord, Rutter, Lavore, & Risi, 1999). The Social Responsiveness Scale is a 65-item questionnaire in which parents rate their child on particular behaviors on a four-point scale, from "not true" to "almost always true," and this measure is quite useful for discriminating whether a child might be on the autism spectrum.

The Autism Diagnostic Observation Schedule is an observation and interview schedule in which a trained interviewer engages in play and conversation with an individual with a view toward rating behavior on a variety of social "presses" (Lord et al., 1999). The child's responses to these semi-structured social presses are rated on a three-point scale; an empirically derived algorithm provides guidelines regarding diagnosis. The authors make it clear that the results provide support for an ASD diagnosis, but the final judgment is a clinical decision. This is a critical point, since administration of the Autism Diagnostic Observation Schedule by a clinician with little knowledge of ASD is not likely to yield valid scores.

The use of these two instruments to measure behavioral change in response to intervention is in the earliest stages of testing. An important limitation is that the ratings for these instruments use a three- to four-point scale, which may not provide enough "spread" to measure incremental but important changes. Further, there needs to be sufficient time between re-administration of these instruments, making them unlikely candidates for addressing progress over shorter intervals (e.g., 6 to 8 weeks).

Some standard instruments are available to measure social skills broadly based, but they have been designed for use with typically developing children and children with other behavioral problems, such as attention-deficit/hyperactivity disorder, oppositional defiant disorder, or shy temperament. The problem is that the atypical behavior associated with ASD may look the same as that of a child with different challenges, but the roots of the problem are not the same. When we look at behavior with a view toward intervention and measurement, we need to consider the function of the behavior, not just the form (Powers, 2005). The danger of using instruments to measure social behavior that have been designed for other populations is that, even if the scores are reliable, it becomes questionable whether the scores or results from that instrument are *valid* for our purposes. The instrument might be recording behavior quite accurately, but the information is misleading. Again, the roots of the social impairment in ASDs are different from the roots of the social impairment in other childhood psychiatric disorders. If interventionists do not understand this, it is not likely that treatment planning will be appropriate.

When designing measurement methods for kids with ASD, usually we are looking for consistent improvement on a particular skill, as well as improvement in social behavior, broadly construed. As described in Chapter 3, the Vineland Adaptive Behavior Scales, second edition (Sparrow et al., 2005) and the Pervasive Developmental Disorders Behavior Inventory (PDD-BI; Cohen & Sudhalter, 2005) may be helpful for gauging longer-term progress. However, they cannot be administered every week. Since the composite scores measure broad growth, there needs to be a sufficient interval between administration of these instruments. For the Vineland, a reasonable interval for re-administration would probably be about 6 months. The PDD-BI can be used in 3-month intervals for very young children since they undergo rapid changes in development compared to older children, whereas for older children the re-administration interval is probably best at 6 to 12 months (I. Cohen, personal communication, 2011).

When working with a particular child, we need something in between for accurate measurement. School teams may devise their own measurement system, based on the format of the IEP they are using and the particulars of what they are trying to measure. The IEP typically requires that evaluation of a behavioral objective be documented and offers a number of possible ways to evaluate progress. An IEP created by a school district may state that the evaluation procedure might include the following:

- Criterion-referenced or curriculum-based assessment
- Standardized assessment
- Baseline data versus post-intervention data
- Behavior or performance rating scale
- Student self-assessment
- Quantitative ratings, with percentage of time performing the behavior as measurement

Clearly, there are a number of ways to evaluate a student's performance, but how many of these methods are reasonable and thoughtful measures of social behavior and increasing social competency? So much depends on how well we are able to precisely describe the behavior that we want the child to learn and to craft a measurement that addresses the core social problem.

Further, the measurement system the team devises must be realistic. It must be easy to use at home, school, or other settings, and include quantitative and qualitative information. Quantitative information is hard data, which may include latency to behavior (the time that elapses), frequency and duration of the behavior, the interval between one behavior and the next time the behavior occurs, or a map of the sequence of behavior. The sequence of behavior would include how often, as well as how quickly, one behavior follows another. Information that can reasonably be counted in this way contributes to overall assessment of progress.

Qualitative information is also important for assessment of progress. This means that impressions, opinions, differing opinions, anecdotes, and varying renditions of what occurred in particular instances should be considered as well. While some believe that qualitative data takes a backseat to quantitative data in measurement, this is not the case. Qualitative information provided by experienced adults working with the child or socially sophisticated children involved with the child may provide background that is not immediately evident when focusing on the concrete details of behavior. These two kinds of information must be thoughtfully integrated to provide the best quality data for assessing progress and modifying treatment methods. IDEA 2004 requires that schools use multiple measures of a child's performance to determine eligibility for services, and this principle should extend to measuring response to treatment.

Essentially, team members must devise measurement strategies that fit the child and the particular behavior and choose a realistic interval for evaluating this information. It may be that a team-created measurement method provides more accurate or detailed information than a commercially prepared measure. This is a time when everyone on the team must provide input about whether they can realistically measure behavior in the setting in which they work. The gym teacher works in a way that is entirely different from the school librarian, the para-professional assigned during math class, or the lunchroom monitor. Everybody has to buy in to conducting measurements and make agreed-upon modifications for their setting that will work. This is also true for the home setting. Expecting a parent to document behavior in 15-minute intervals throughout the day just is not a viable plan. In any case, multiple measurements should be used to assess how a child is progressing. This is the best way to get a well-rounded picture of the child's functioning.

DIRECT OBSERVATION

Observing a child directly is an excellent method for determining whether skills and new behaviors are coming online. With direct observation, the criteria for considering that a behavior is present or absent must be very clear, and the biases of all observers and raters must be out in the open. It is nearly impossible not to have some sort of bias about how the child might behave if you are a team member working with the child. In research studies, observers and raters are usually blinded to the treatment condition, so they are performing ratings about behavior with no knowledge of whether the child is involved in treatment or in a control (non-treatment) group. It is unlikely that blind ratings could work in a school or community setting, when the parents and professionals are fully aware of the intervention in place. Nevertheless, direct observation can be tremendously useful for understanding not only how the child does or does not fit in socially with peers but also how the peer group interacts with one another and with the child with ASD. As noted in Chapter 1, peer groups or cliques have their own unspoken rules for what kind of behavior is acceptable, and the school team are insiders with regard to knowing what happens and how to interpret social interaction in their setting.

LEGAL ISSUES

It is important to consider that the issues surrounding accurate measurement and the documentation of progress may become part of a legal process at some point. While families and school districts prefer not to bring disputes about the effectiveness of treatment to that point, it sometimes happens. Clearly, methods of measurement must be well outlined and procedures followed correctly, primarily to promote effective treatment of the child, but also to abide by legal requirements for documentation as described in IDEA 2004. The language in IDEA 2004 requires that evaluations, not only for initial eligibility but also for progress, include "a variety of assessment tools and strategies to gather relevant functional, developmental, and academic information" and that the local educational agency "not use any single measure or assessment as the sole criterion . . . for determining an appropriate educational placement for the child" [20 U.S.C. §1414 (b)(2) (A) (B)]. Again, this standard should be considered as a guideline for determining progress. We should not count on any one assessment tool or observation to give us the full picture of the child's behavior and progress. In fact, the assessment tool that works best is one that gives us information about what might be deterring progress, so the team can tweak the program to address the issue.

WHAT DO WE CONSIDER SUCCESS?

In the end, the team, including school professionals, community professionals, and family, should consider what social success truly means for a particular child. For many children, having one real friend to spend time with and confide in is all that is needed to be content and feel good about social relationships. We want the child to experience the warmth and emotional connection of a friendship, since this is what provides the child with confidence, security, and the courage to grow. At times, families must scale down their expectations for what success means. We have run across families in which success is defined as being popular among peers—a nearly unreachable goal for a child with ASD—or being a leader in sports or other extracurricular activities. In these situations, we have to consider whether the child's social success is gauged by what is meaningful for the child or what is meaningful for the adults. Sometimes school or community professionals may need to help parents understand what is realistic and what is meaningful. This is not always easy given the expectations families have for their children, and it may be a process that the family and team members go through over time as they learn what the child is capable of and what may beyond his reach. Essentially, children and adolescents with ASD can lead meaningful, productive, and personally satisfying lives, with enriching social relationships, although this may look different from what we as interventionists envisioned at the start.

Readings and Resources

• •

Carter, E., Cushing, L., & Kennedy, C. (2000). *Peer support strategies for improving all students' social lives and learning.* Baltimore, MD: Paul Brookes.

Cohen, M., & Sloan, D. (2007). *Visual supports for people with autism.* Bethesda, MD: Woodbine House.

Hodgdon, L. (2001). *Visual strategies for improving communication.* Troy, MI: Quirk Roberts.

Koegel, R. L., & Koegel, L. K. (2006). *Pivotal response treatments for autism: Communication, social and academic development.* Baltimore, MD: Paul Brookes.

National Research Council. (2001). *Educating children with autism.* Washington, DC: National Academy Press.

Quill, K. (2000). *Do-watch-listen-say: Social and communication intervention for children with autism.* Baltimore, MD: Paul Brookes.

Rogers, S., & Dawson, G. (2010). *Early start Denver model for young children with autism.* New York: Guilford.

Volkmar, F., & Weisner, L. (2009). *A practical guide to autism: What every parent, family member and teacher needs to know.* Hoboken, NJ: Wiley.

Wright, P., & Wright, P. (2007). *Special education law* (2nd ed.). Hartfield, VA: Harbour House Law Press.

References

Aldred, C., Green, T., & Adams, C. (2004). A new social communication intervention for a child with autism: Pilot randomized controlled treatment study suggesting effectiveness. *Journal of Child Psychology and Psychiatry, 45,* 1420–1430.

Aldred, C., Pollard, C., & Adams, C. (2001). Child's talk—for children with autism and pervasive developmental disorder. *International Journal of Language and Communication Disorders, 36*(suppl.), 469–474.

American Psychiatric Association. (2000). *Diagnostic and statistical manual of mental disorders* (4th ed., text rev.). Washington, DC: Author.

Angelesea, M., Hoch, H., & Taylor, B. (2008). Reduced rapid eating in teenagers with autism: Use of a pager prompt. *Journal of Applied Behavior Analysis, 41,* 107–111.

Apple, L., Billingsly, F., & Schwartz, I. (2005). Effects of video modeling alone and with self-management on compliment giving behaviors of children with high-functioning ASD. *Journal of Positive Behavior Interventions, 7*(1), 33–47.

Aspy, R., & Grossman, B. (2008). *Designing comprehensive interventions for individuals with high functioning and Asperger syndrome: The Ziggurat model* (textbook ed.). Shawnee Mission, KS: Autism Asperger.

Ayres, K. M., & Langone, J. (2005). Intervention and instruction with video for students with autism: A review of the literature. *Education and Training in Mental Retardation and Developmental Disabilities, 40*(2), 183–196.

Bailey, K. (2008). Supporting families. In K. Chawarska, A. Klin, & F. Volkmar (Eds.), *Autism spectrum disorders in infants and tddlers: Diagnosis, assessment and treatment* (pp. 300–326). New York: Guilford.

Baker, J. (2003). *Social skills training for children and adolescents with As-*

perger syndrome and social communication problems. Shawnee Mission, KS: Autism Asperger.

Baker-Ericzén, M., Brookman-Frazee, L., & Stahmer, A. (2005). Stress levels and adaptability in parents of toddlers with and without autism spectrum disorders. *Research and Practice for Persons with Severe Disabilities, 30*(4), 194–204.

Barnhill, G., Tapscott Cook, K., Tebbenkamp, K., & Smith-Myles, B. (2002). The effectiveness of social skills intervention targeting nonverbal communication for adolescents with Asperger syndrome and related pervasive developmental delays. *Focus on Autism and Other Developmental Disabilities, 17*(2), 112–118.

Barron, A., & Foot, H. (1991). Peer tutoring and tutor training. *Educational Research, 33,* 174–185.

Barry, C., & Wigfield, A. (2002). Friendship making ability and perceptions of friend's deviant behavior: Childhood to adolescence. *Journal of Early Adolescence, 22,* 143–172.

Barry, T. D., Klinger, L. G., Lee, J. M., Palardy, N., Gilmore, T., & Bodin, S. D. (2003). Examining the effectiveness of an outpatient clinic-based social skills group for high-functioning children with autism. *Journal of Autism and Developmental Disorders, 33,* 685–701.

Bauminger, N. (2007). Brief report: Individual social-multi-modal intervention for HFASD. *Journal of Autism and Developmental Disorders, 37,* 1593–1604.

Bauminger, N., & Kasari, C. (2000). Loneliness and friendship in high-functioning children with autism. *Child Development, 71*(2), 447–456.

Bellini, S. (2008). *Building social relationships: A systematic approach to teaching social interaction skills to children and adolescents with autism spectrum and other social disabilities.* Shawnee Mission, KS: Autism Asperger.

Bellini, S., & Peters, J. K. (2008). Social skills training for youth with autism spectrum disorders. *Child and Adolescent Psychiatric Clinics of North America, 17*(4), 857.

Benson, J., & Sabbagh, M. (2010). Theory of mind and executive functioning. In P. Zelazo, M. Chandler, & E. Crone (Eds.), *Developmental social cognitive neuroscience* (pp. 63-80). New York: Psychology Press/Taylor and Francis.

Benson, P. R., & Karlof, K. L. (2008). Child, parent, and family predictors of latter adjustment in siblings of children with autism. *Research in Autism Spectrum Disorders, 2,* 583–600.

Berndt, T., Hawkins, J., & Jiao, Z. (1999). Influences of friends and friendships on adjustment to junior high school. *Merrill-Palmer Quarterly, 45,* 12–41.

Betz, A. M., Higbee, T. S., & Reagon, K. A. (2008). Using joint activity schedules to promote peer engagement in preschoolers with autism. *Journal of Applied Behavior Analysis, 41,* 237–241.

Bibock, M., Carpendale, J., & Müller, U. (2009). Parental scaffolding and the development of executive functioning. *New Directions in Child and Adolescent Development, 123,* 17–34.

Bishop, S., Luyster, R., Richler, J., & Lord, C. (2008). Diagnostic assessment. In K. Chawarska, A. Klin, & F. R. Volkmar (Eds.), *Autism spectrum disorders in infants and toddlers* (pp. 23–49). New York: Guilford.

Bolte, S., Golan, O., Goodwin, M., & Zwaigenbaum, L. (2010). What can innovative technologies do for autism spectrum disorders? *Autism, 143*(3), 155–159.

Boutot, E. A. (2009). Using "I will" cards and social coaches to improve social behaviors of students with Asperger syndrome. *Intervention in School and Clinic, 44*(5), 276–281.

Boutot, E. A., Guenther, T., & Crozier, S. (2005). Let's play: Teaching play skills to young children with autism. *Education and Training in Developmental Disabilities, 40,* 285–292.

Boyd, B. (2002). Examining the relationship between stress and lack of social support in mothers of children with autism. *Focus on Autism and Other Developmental Disabilities, 17*(4), 208–215.

Bregman, J., Zager, D., & Gerdtz, J. (2005). Behavioral interventions. In F. Volkmar, R. Paul, A. Klin, & D. Cohen (Eds.), *Handbook of autism and pervasive developmental disorders* (3rd ed., Vol. 2, pp. 897–924). Hoboken, NJ: Wiley.

Brier, N. (1995). Predicting antisocial behavior in youngsters displaying poor academic achievement: A review of risk factors. *Developmental and Behavioral Pediatrics, 16*(4), 271–276.

Calkins, S., & Marcovitch, S. (2010). Emotion regulation and executive functioning in early development: Integrated mechanisms of control support adaptive functioning. In S. Calkins & M. A. Bell (Eds.), *Child development at the intersection of emotion and cognition* (pp. 37–58). Washington, DC: American Psychological Association.

Campbell, J. (2006). Changing children's attitudes toward autism: A process of persuasive communication. *Journal of Developmental and Physical Disabilities, 18*(3), 251–272.

REFERENCES

Carlson, S. (2009). Social origins of executive function development. *New Directions in Child and Adolescent Development*, *123*, 87–98.

Carter, A. S., Davis, N. O., Klin, A., & Volkmar, F. R. (2005). Social Development in Autism. In F. R. Volkmar, A. Klin, R. Paul & D. J. Cohen (Eds.), *Handbook of Autism and Pervasive Developmental Disorders* (3rd ed., Vol. 1, pp. 312-334). Hoboken, NJ: Wiley.

Carter, E., Cushing, L., Clark, N., & Kennedy, C. (2005). Effects of peer support interventions on students' access to the general curriculum and social interactions. *Research and Practice for Persons with Severe Disabilities*, *30*(1), 15–25.

Carter, E., Cushing, L., & Kennedy, C. (2009). *Peer support strategies for improving all students' social lives and learning.* Baltimore, MD: Paul Brookes.

Carter, E., & Hughes, C. (2005). Increasing social interaction among adolescents with intellectual disabilities and their general education peers: Effective interventions. *Research and Practice for Persons with Severe Disabilities*, *30*(4), 179–193.

Chan, J. M., & O'Reilly, M. (2008). A Social Stories™ intervention package for students with autism in inclusive classroom settings. *Journal of Applied Behavior Analysis*, *41*(3), 405–409.

Chalfant, A., Rapee, R., & Carroll, L. (2007). Treating anxiety disorders in children with high functioning autism spectrum disorders: A controlled trial. *Journal of Autism and Developmental Disorders*, *37*, 1842–1857.

Charlop, M., & Milstein, J. (1989). Teaching autistic children conversational speech using video modeling. *Journal of Applied Behavior Analysis*, *22*(3), 275–285.

Charlop-Cristy, M., Le, L., & Freeman, J. (2000). A comparison of video modeling with in vivo modeling for teaching children with autism. *Journal of Autism and Developmental Disorders*, *30*, 537–552.

Chawarska, K., & Volkmar, F. (2005). Autism in infancy and early childhood. In: F. Volkmar, A. Klin, & R. Paul (Eds.), *Handbook of autism and developmental disorders* (3rd ed., pp. 223–246). New York: Wiley.

Chung, K., Reavis, S., Mosconi, M., Drewry, J., Matthews, T., & Tasse, M. (2007). Peer mediated social skills training programs for young children with high functioning autism. *Research in Developmental Disabilities*, *28*(4), 423–436.

Cohen, I. (2003). Criterion-related validity of the PDD-Behavior Inventory. *Journal of Autism and Developmental Disorders*, *33*, 47–53.

Cohen, I., Schmidt-Lackner, S., Romanczyk, R., & Sudhalter, V. (2003). The

PDD-Behavior Inventory: A rating scale for assessing response to intervention in children with pervasive developmental disorder. *Journal of Autism and Developmental Disorders, 33,* 31–45.

Cohen, I., & Sudhalter, V. (2005). *PDD-BI Behavior Inventory: Professional manual.* Lutz, FL: Psychological Assessment Resources.

Cohen, M., & Sloan, D. (2007). *Visual supports for people with autism: A guide for parents and professionals.* Bethesda, MD: Woodbine House.

Cole, P., Armstrong, L., & Pemberton, C. (2010). The role of language in the development of emotion regulation. In S. Calkins & M. A. Bell (Eds.), *Child development at the intersection of emotion and cognition* (pp. 59–78). Washington, DC: American Psychological Association.

Constantino, J., & Gruber, C. (2005). *The Social Responsiveness Scale.* Los Angeles: Western Psychological Services.

Cotugno, A. (2009). Social competence and social skills training and intervention for children with autism spectrum disorders. *Journal of Autism and Developmental Disorders, 39,* 1268–1277.

Coucouvanis, J. (2005). *Super skills: A social sills group program for children with Asperger syndrome, high-functioning autism and related challenges.* Shawnee Mission, KS: Autism Asperger.

Crozier, S., & Tincani, M. (2007). Effects of social stories on prosocial behavior of preschool children with autism spectrum disorders. *Journal of Autism and Developmental Disorders, 37,* 1803–1814.

Darden-Brunson, F., Green, A., & Goldstein, H. (2010). Video-based instruction for children with autism. In J. Luiselli, D. Russo, W. Christian, & S. Wilcynski (Eds.), *Effective practices for children with autism: Educational and behavioral support interventions that work* (pp. 241–268). New York: Oxford University Press.

Delano, M., & Snell, M. E. (2006). The effects of social stories on the social engagement of children with autism. *Journal of Positive Behavior Intervention, 8,* 29–42.

De Los Reyes, A., & Kazdin, A. E. (2005). Informant discrepancies in the assessment of childhood psychopathology: A critical review, theoretical framework, and recommendations for further study. *Psychological Bulletin, 131*(4), 483–509.

Dunn, M., Burbine, R., Bowers, C., & Tanteleff-Dunn, S. (2001). Moderators of stress in parents of children with autism. *Community Mental Health Journal, 37*(1), 39–52.

DuPaul, G.J., Ervin, R., Hook, C. & McGoey, K. (1998). Peer tutoring for children with attention deficit hyperactivity disorder: Effects on classroom behavior and academic performance. *Journal of Applied Behavior Analysis, 31(4),* 579-592.

Eisenberg, N., Fabes, R., Karbon, L., Murphy, B., Carlo, G., & Wonsonski, M. (1996). Relations of school children's comforting behavior to empathy-related reactions and shyness. *Social Development, 5*(3), 330–351.

Ferraioli, S., & Harris, S. (2011). Treatments to increase social awareness and social skills. In B. Reichow, P. Doering, D. Cicchetti, & F. Volkmar (Eds.), *Evidence-based practices and treatments for children with autism* (pp. 171–196). New York: Springer.

Frankel, F., & Myatt, R. (2003). *Children's friendship training.* New York: Brunner-Routledge.

Ganz, J. B., & Flores, M. (2008). Effects of the use of visual strategies in play groups for children with autism spectrum disorders and their peers. *Journal of Autism and Developmental Disorders, 38,* 926–940.

Ganz, J. B., Simpson, R. L., & Corbin-Newsome, J. (2008). The impact of the Picture Exchange Communication System on requesting and speech development in preschoolers with autism spectrum disorders and similar characteristics. *Research in Autism Spectrum Disorders, 2*(1), 157–169.

Gena, A., Coulora, S., & Kysmiss, E. (2005). Modifying the affective behavior of preschoolers with autism using in-vivo or video-modeling and reinforcement contingencies. *Journal of Autism and Developmental Disorders, 35*(5), 545–556.

Gerhardt, P. (2009). Transition to adulthood for learners with ASD. http://www.youtube.com/. Retrieved 2011.

Ghezzi, P., & Bishop, M. (2008). Generalized behavior change in young children with autism. In J. Luiselli, D. Russo, W. Christian, & S. Wilcynski (Eds.), *Effective practices for children with autism: Educational and behavioral support interventions that work.* New York: Oxford University Press.

Gillett, J. N., & LeBlanc, L. A. (2007). Parent-implemented natural language paradigm to increase language and play in children with autism. *Research in Autism Spectrum Disorders, 1*(3), 247–255.

Goldstein, H., & Cisar, C. (1992). Promoting interaction during sociodramatic play: Teaching scripts to typical preschoolers and classmates with disabilities. *Journal of Applied Behavior Analysis, 25,* 265–280.

Goldstein, H., Kaczmarek, L., Pennington, R., & Shafer, K. (1992). Peer-mediated intervention: Attending to, commenting on, and acknowledging the behavior of preschoolers with autism. *Journal of Applied Behavior Analysis, 25,* 289–305.

Gray, C. (2000). *The new social story book: Illustrated edition.* Arlington, TX: Future Horizons.

Gray, C., & Gerand, J. (1993). Social stories: Improving responses of students with autism with accurate social information. *Focus on Autistic Behavior, 81*(1), 1–10.

Gumpel, T., & Frank, R. (1999). An expansion of the peer tutoring paradigm: Cross-age peer tutoring of social skills among socially rejected boys. *Journal of Applied Behavior Analysis, 32,* 115–118.

Hale, J. (2008). Response to intervention: Guidelines for parents and practitioners. http://www.wrightslaw.com. Retrieved 2011.

Hastings, R. (2003). Child behavior problems and partner mental health as correlates of stress in mothers and fathers of children with autism. *Journal of Intellectual Disability Research, 47*(4/5), 231–237.

Hastings, R. (2010). Stress in parents of children with autism. In E. MacGregor, M. Núñez, K. Cebula, & J. C. Gómez (Eds.), *Autism: An integrated view from neurocognitive, clinical, and intervention research.* Malden, MA: Blackwell.

Hastings, R., & Beck, A. (2004). Practitioner review: Stress intervention for parents of children with intellectual disabilities. *Journal of Child Psychology and Psychiatry, 45*(8), 1338–1349.

Hess, L. (2006). I would like to play but I don't know how: A case study of pretend play in autism. *Child Language Teaching and Therapy, 22*(1), 97–116.

Hoch, H., Taylor, B., & Rodriguez, A. (2009). Teaching teenagers with autism to answer cell phones and seek assistance when lost. *Behavior Analysis in Practice, 2,* 2–7.

Howlin, P., Mawhood, L., & Rutter, M. (2000). Autism and developmental receptive language disorder—a follow up comparison in early adult life. II: Social, behavioural and psychiatric outcomes. *Journal of Child Psychology and Psychiatry, 41*(5), 561–578.

Hughes, C., Copeland, S., Wehmeyer, M., Agran, M., Cai, X., & Hwang, B. (2002). Increasing social interaction between general education high school students and their peers with mental retardation. *Journal of Developmental and Physical Disabilities, 14*(4), 387–402.

Hume, K., Loftin, R., & Lantz, J. (2009). Increasing independence in autism spectrum disorders: A review of three focused interventions. *Journal of Autism and Developmental Disorders, 39,* 1329–1338.

Individuals With Disabilities Education Act, 20 U.S.C. §1400 et seq. 2004.

Ingersoll, B. (2008). The effect of context on imitation skills in children with autism. *Research in Autism Spectrum Disorders, 2*(2), 332–340.

REFERENCES

Interagency Autism Coordinating Committee. (2011). 2011 strategic plan for autism spectrum disorder research. http://www.iacc.hhs.gov.

Jennings, P., & Greenberg, M. (2009). The prosocial classroom: Teacher social and emotional competence in relation to student and classroom outcomes. *Review of Educational Research, 79*(1), 491–525.

Jones, E. A. (2009). Establishing response and stimulus classes for initiating joint attention in children with autism. *Research in Autism Spectrum Disorders, 3*(2), 375–389.

Jones, W., & Klin, A. (2008). Altered salience in autism: Developmental insights, consequences and questions. In E. McGregor, M. Núñez, K. Cebula, & J. Gómez (Eds.), *Autism: An integrated view from neurocognitive, clinical, and intervention research* (pp. 62–82). Malden, MA: Blackwell.

Kaiser, M. D., Hudac, C. M., Shultz, S., Lee, S. M., Cheung, C., Berken, A. M., . . . Pelphrey, K. A. (2010). Neural signatures of autism. [Research Support, Non-U.S. Gov't]. *Proceedings of the National Academy of Sciences of the United States of America, 107*(49), 21223-21228.

Kamps, D., & Garrison-Harrell, L. (1997). The effects of peer network on social-communicative behaviors for students with autism. *Focus on Autism and Other Developmental Disabilities, 12*, 241–254.

Kanner, L. (1943). Autistic disturbances of affective contact. *Nervous Child, 2*, 217-250.

Karreman, A., van Tuijl, C., van Aken, M., & Dekovic, M. (2006). Parenting and self-regulation in preschoolers: A meta-analysis. *Infant and Child Development, 15*, 561–579.

Kasari, C., Freeman, S., & Paparella, T. (2006). Joint attention and symbolic play in young children with autism: A randomized controlled intervention study. *Journal of Child Psychology and Psychiatry and Allied Disciplines, 47*, 611–620. [Erratum in *Journal of Child Psychology and Psychiatry, 2007, 48*, 523].

Kasari, C., Gulsrud, A., Wong, C., Kwon, S., & Locke, J. (2010). Randomized controlled caregiver mediated joint attention intervention for toddlers with autism. *Journal of Autism and Developmental Disorders*, published online: February 10.

Kaufman, A., & Kaufman, N. (2005). *Kaufman brief intelligence test* (2nd ed.). Los Angeles: Western Psychological Services.

Klin, A., Jones, W., Schultz, R., Volkmar, F., & Cohen, D. (2002). Defining and quantifying the social phenotype in autism. *American Journal of Psychiatry, 159*(6), 895-908.

Klin, A., Saulnier, C., Sparrow, S., Cicchetti, D., Volkmar, F. R., & Lord, C.

214

(2007). Social and communication abilities and disabilities in higher functioning individuals with autism spectrum disorders: The Vineland and the ADOS. *Journal of Autism and Developmental Disorders, 37,* 748–759.

Klin, A., Saulnier, C., Tsatsanis, K., & Volkmar, F. R. (2005). Clinical evaluation in autism spectrum disorders: Psychological assessment within a transdisciplinary framework. In F. R. Volkmar, R. Paul, A. Klin, & D. Cohen (Eds.), *Handbook of autism and pervasive developmental disorders: Assessment, interventions and policy* (3rd ed., Vol. 2, pp. 772–798). Hoboken, NJ: Wiley.

Koegel, R., & and Koegel, L. (1995). *Teaching children with autism: Strategies for initiating positive interactions and improving learning opportunities.* Baltimore, MD: Paul H. Brookes.

Koegel, R., & Kern Koegel, L. (2006). *Pivotal response treatments for autism: Communication, social and academic development.* Baltimore, MD: Paul Brookes.

Koegel, R., Koegel, L., & Brookman, L. (2003). Empirically supported pivotal response interventions for children with autism. In A. Kazdin & J. R. Weisz (Eds.), *Evidence-based psychotherapies for children and adolescents* (pp. 341–357). New York: Guilford.

Koegel, R., Koegel, L. K., & Camarata, S. (2010). Definitions of empirically supported treatment. *Journal of Autism and Developmental Disorders, 40,* 516–517.

Koegel, R., Koegel, L., Vernon, T., & Brookman-Frazee, L. (2010). Empirically supported pivotal response treatment for children with autism spectrum disorders. In J. Weitz, A. Kazdin, P. Chamberlain, D. Smith, & B. Chorpita (Eds.), *Evidence-based psychotherapies for children and adolescents* (2nd ed., p. 327). New York: Guilford.

Koegel, R., Schreibman, L., Loos, L., Dirlech-Wilhelm, H., Dunlap, G., Robbins, F., & Plienis, M. (1992). Consistent stress profiles in mothers of children with autism. *Journal of Autism and Developmental Disorders, 22*(2), 205–216.

Koenig, K., De Los Reyes, A., Cicchetti, D., Scahill, L., & Klin, A. (2009). Group intervention to promote social skills in school-age children with pervasive developmental disorders: Reconsidering efficacy. *Journal of Autism and Developmental Disorders, 39,* 1163–1172.

Koenig, K., & Levine, M. (2011). Psychotherapy for individuals with autism spectrum disorders. *Journal of Contemporary Psychotherapy, 41,* 29–36.

Koenig, K., & Tsatsanis, K. (2005). Pervasive developmental disorders in girls. In D. Bell, S. L. Foster, & E. J. Mash (Eds.), *Handbook of behavioral and emotional problems in girls* (pp. 211–237). New York: Kluwer Academic/Plenum.

Koenig, K., Williams White, S., Pachler, M., Lau, M., Lewis, M., Klin, A., & Scahill, L. (2010). Promoting social skill development in children with pervasive development disorders: A feasibility and efficacy study. *Journal of Autism and Developmental Disorders, 40*, 1209–1218.

Kokina, A., & Kern, L. (2010). Social Story™ interventions for students with autism spectrum disorders: A meta-analysis. *Journal of Autism and Developmental Disorders*, published online: January 7.

Krantz, P. J., & McClannahan, L. E. (1993). Teaching children with autism to initiate to peers: Effects of a script fading procedure. *Journal of Applied Behavior Analysis, 26*, 121–132.

Krantz, P. & McClannahan, L. (1998). Social interaction skills for children with autism: A script-fading procedure. *Journal of Applied Behavior Analysis, 31(2)*, 191-202.

Kroeger, K., Schultz, J., & Newsom, C. (2007). A comparison of two group-delivered social skills programs for young children with autism. *Journal of Autism and Developmental Disorders, 37*, 808–817.

Kuhn, J. & Carter, A. (2006). Maternal self-efficacy and associated parenting cognitions among mothers of children with autism. *American Journal of Orthopsychiatry, 76 (4)*, 564-575.

Landry, S., Smith, K., & Swank, P. (2009). New directions in evaluating social problem solving in childhood: Early precursors and links to adolescent social competence. *New Directions in Child and Adolescent Development, 123*, 51–68.

Laugeson, E. A., Frankel, F., Mogil, C., & Dillon, A. R. (2009). Parent-assisted social skills training to improve friendships in teens with autism spectrum disorders. *Journal of Autism and Developmental Disorders, 39*, 596–606.

Laushey, K., & Helflin, L. J. (2000). Enhancing social skills of kindergarten children with autism through the training of multiple peers as tutors. *Journal of Autism and Developmental Disorders, 30*, 183–193.

LeBlanc, L., Coates, A., Daneshvar, S., Charlop-Christy, M., Morris, C., & Lancaster, B. (2003). Using video modeling and reinforcement to teach perspective-taking skills to children with autism. *Journal of Applied Behavior Analysis, 36*, 253–257.

Lerner, M., & Levine, K. (2007). The Spotlight Program: An integrative ap-

216

proach to teaching social pragmatics using dramatic principles and techniques. *Journal of Developmental Processes, 2*(2), 91–102.

Lerner, M., Mikami, A., & McLeod, B. (2011). The alliance in a friendship coaching intervention for parents of children with ADHD. *Behavior Therapy, 42,* 449–461.

Lewis, C., & Carpendale, J. (2009). Introduction: Links between social interaction and executive functioning. *New Directions in Child and Adolescent Development, 123,* 1–16.

Litris, S., Moore, D., & Anderson, A. (2010). Using video self-modelled social stories to teach social skills to a young child with autism. *Autism Research and Treatment,* 1–9. doi:10.1155/2010/834979

Litvack-Miller, W., McDougall, D., & Romney, D. (1997). The structure of empathy during middle childhood and its relationship to prosocial behavior. *Genetic, Social and General Psychology Monographs, 123*(3), 303–324.

Locke, J., Ishijima, E., Kasari, C., & London, N. (2010). Loneliness, friendship quality, and the social networks of adolescents with high-functioning autism in an inclusive school setting. *Journal of Research in Special Educational Needs, 10*(2), 74–81.

Loomis, J. (2008). *Staying in the game: Promoting social opportunities for children and adolescents with autism spectrum disorders and other development disabilities.* Shawnee Mission, KS: Autism Asperger.

Lopata, C., Thomeer, M., Volker, M., Nida, R., & Lee, G. (2008). Effectiveness of a manualized summer social treatment program for high-functioning children with autism spectrum disorders. *Journal of Autism and Developmental Disorders, 38,* 890–904.

Lord, C., Rutter, M., DiLavore, P. C., & Risi, S. (1999). *Autism Diagnostic Observation Schedule.* Los Angeles, CA: Western Psychological Services.

Lord, C., Risi, S., Lambrecht, L., Cook, E. H., Leventhal, B. L., DiLavore, P. C., et al. (2000). The Autism Diagnostic Observation Schedule-Generic: A standard measure of social and communication deficits associated with the spectrum of autism. *Journal of Autism and Developmental Disorders, 30,* 205–223.

Loth, E. (2008). Abnormalities in "cultural knowledge" in autism spectrum disorders: A link between behavior and cognition. In E. McGregor, M. Núñez, K. Cebula, & J. Gómez (Eds.), *Autism: An integrated view from neurocognitive, clinical and intervention research* (pp. 83–103). Malden, MA: Blackwell.

REFERENCES

Lovaas, O. I. (1987). Behavioral treatment and normal educational and intellectual functioning in young autistic children. *Journal of Consulting and Clinical Psychology,55*, 3-9.

Lovaas, O., & Smith, T. (1988). Intensive behavioral treatment for young autistic children In Benjamin B. Lahey and Alan E. Kazdin (Eds.), *Advances in clinical child psychology, Vol 11* (pp 285–324).

MacDonald, R., Sacramones, S., Mansfield, R., Wiltz, K., & Ahern, W. H. (2009). Using video modeling to teach reciprocal pretend play to children with autism. *Journal of Applied Behavior Analysis, 42*, 43–55.

MacKay, T., Knott, F., & Dunlop, A. W. (2007). Developing social interaction and understanding in individuals with autism spectrum disorder: A groupwork intervention. *Journal of Intellectual and Developmental Disability, 32*(4), 279–290.

Mak, W., Ho, A., & Law, R. (2007). Sense of coherence, parenting attitudes and stress among mothers of children with autism in Hong Kong. *Journal of Applied Research in Intellectual Disabilities, 20*, 157–167.

Martin, G., & Pear, J. (1988). *Behavior modification: What it is and how to do it* (3rd ed.). Englewood Cliffs, NJ: Prentice Hall.

McCathren, R. (2000). Teacher-implemented communication intervention. *Focus on Autism and Other Developmental Disabilities, 15*(1), 21–29.

McEachen, J., Smith, T., & Lovaas, O. (1993). Long-term outcome for children with autism who received early intensive behavioral treatment. *American Journal on Mental Retardation, 97*, 359–372.

McEvoy, A., & Welker, R. (2000). Antisocial behavior, academic failure and school climate: A critical review. *Journal of Emotional and Behavioral Disorders, 8*(3), 130–140.

Meirsschaut, M., Roeyers, H., & Warreyn, P. (2010). Parenting in families with a child with autism spectrum disorder and a typically developing child: Mothers' experiences and cognitions. *Research in Autism Spectrum Disorders, 4*, 661–669.

Merrell, K. (1999). *Behavioral, social and emotional assessment of children and adolescents.* Mahwah, NJ: Erlbaum.

Mikami, A., Lerner, M., & Lun, J. (2010). Social context influences on children's rejection by their peers. *Child Development Perspectives, 4*(2), 123–130.

Millar, D. C., Light, J. C., & Schossler, R. (2006). The impact of augmentative and alternative communication intervention on the speech production of individuals with developmental disabilities: A research review. *Journal of Speech, Language and Hearing Research, 49*, 248–264.

Moree, B. N., & Davis, T. E. (2010). Cognitive-behavioral therapy for anxiety in children diagnosed with autism spectrum disorders: Modification trends. *Research in Autism Spectrum Disorders, 4*(3), 346-354.

Morrison, F., Cameron Ponitz, C., & McClelland, M. (2010). Self-regulation and academic achievement in the transition to school. In S. D. Calkins & M. A. Bell (Eds.), *Child development at the intersection of emotion and cognition* (pp. 203–224). Washington, DC: American Psychological Association.

Morrison, L., Kamps, D., Garcia, J., & Parker, D. (2001). Peer mediation and monitoring strategies to improve initiations and social skills for students with autism. *Journal of Positive Behavior Interventions, 3*(4), 237–250.

National Research Council. (2001). *Educating children with autism.* Washington, DC: National Academy Press.

Nikopoulos, C. K., & Keenan, M. (2003). Promoting social initiation in children with autism using video modeling. *Behavioral Interventions, 18*(2), 87–108.

No Child Left Behind Act. (2001). Public Law 107-110.

Odom, S., Boyd, B., Hall, L., & Hume, K. (2010). Evaluation of comprehensive treatment models for individuals with autism spectrum disorders. *Journal of Autism and Developmental Disorders, 40*, 425–436.

Odom, S., & Strain, P. (1984). Peer-mediated approaches to promoting children's social interaction: A review. *American Journal of Orthopsychiatry, 54*, 544–557.

Odom, S., & Strain, P. (1986). A comparison of peer initiation and teacher antecedent interventions for promoting reciprocal social interaction of autistic preschoolers. *Journal of Applied Behavioral Analysis, 19*, 59–67.

Ogletree, B. T., Oren, T., & Fischer, M. A. (2007). Examining effective intervention practices for communication impairment in autism spectrum disorder. *Exceptionality, 15*(4), 233–247.

Orvalho, V., Miranda, J., & Sousa, A. (2009). Facial synthesis of 3D avatars for therapeutic applications. *Annual Review of Cybertherapy and Telemedicine, 7*, 96–98.

Osborne, L. A., & Reed, P. (2010). Stress and self-perceived parenting behaviors of parents of children with autistic spectrum conditions. *Research in Autism Spectrum Disorders, 4*(3), 405–414.

Ozonoff, S., & Miller, J. (1995). Teaching theory of mind: A new approach to social skills training for individuals with autism. *Journal of Autism and Developmental Disorders, 25*, 415–433.

REFERENCES

Parker, J., & Asher, S. (1993). Friendship and friendship quality in middle childhood: Links with peer group acceptance and feelings of loneliness and social dissatisfaction. *Developmental Psychology, 29*, 611–621.

Paul, R. (2003). Promoting social communication in high functioning individuals with autistic spectrum disorders. *Child and Adolescent Psychiatric Clinics of North America, 12*, 87–106.

Paul, R. (2008a). Communication development and assessment. In K. Chawarska, A. Klin, & F. R. Volkmar (Eds.), *Autism spectrum disorders in infants and toddlers* (pp. 76–103). New York: Guilford.

Paul, R. (2008b). Interventions to improve communication in autism. *Child and Adolescent Psychiatric Clinics of North America, 17*, 835–856.

Peterson, P. (2009). Promoting generalization and maintenance of skills learned via natural language teaching. *Journal of Speech-Language Pathology and Applied Behavior Analysis, 4*, 90–131.

Pettursdottir, A., McComas, J., McMaster, K., & Horner, K. (2007). The effects of scripted peer tutors and programming common stimuli on social interactions of a student with autism spectrum disorders. *Journal of Applied Behavior Analysis, 40*(2), 353–357.

Pierce, K., & Schreibman, L. (1995). Increasing complex social behaviors in children with autism: Effects of peer-implemented pivotal response training. *Journal of Applied Behavior Analysis, 28*, 285–295.

Pierce, K., & Schreibman, L. (1997). Multiple peer use of pivotal response training to increase social behaviors of classmates with autism: Results from trained and untrained peers. *Journal of Applied Behavior Analysis, 30*, 157–160.

Ploog, B. O., Banerjee, S., & Brooks, P. J. (2009). Attention to prosody (intonation) and content in children with autism and in typical children using spoken sentences in a computer game. *Research in Autism Spectrum Disorders, 3*, 743–758.

Powers, M. (2005). Behavioral assessment of individuals with autism: A functional ecological approach. In F. Volkmar, A. Klin, R. Paul, & D. Cohen, (Eds.), *Handbook of autism and developmental disorders* (3rd ed., pp. 817–830). New York: Wiley.

Prendeville, J. A., Prelock, P. A., & Unwin, G. (2006). Peer play interventions to support the social competence of children with autism spectrum disorders. *Seminars in Speech and Language, 27*(1), 32–45.

Preston, D., & Carter, M. (2009). A review of the efficacy of the picture exchange communication system intervention. *Journal of Autism and Developmental Disorders, 39*, 1471–1486.

Prizant, B., & Wetherby, A. (1998). Understanding the continuum of discrete-trial traditional behavioral to social-pragmatic developmental approaches in communication enhancement for young children with autism/PDD. *Seminars in Speech and Language, 19*(4), 329–353.

Prizant, B., Wetherby, A., Rubin, E., & Laurent, A. (2003). The SCERTS Model: A transactional, family centered approach to enhancing communication and socioemotional abilities of children with autism spectrum disorders. *Infants and Young Children, 16*, 296–316.

Quill, K. (2000). *Do-watch-listen-say: Social and communication intervention for children with autism*. Baltimore, MD: Paul Brookes.

Quirmbach, L. M., Lincoln, A. J., Feinberg-Gizzo, M. J., Ingersoll, B. R., & Andrews, S. (2009). Social stories: Mechanisms of effectiveness in increasing game play skills in children diagnosed with autism spectrum disorder using a pretest-posttest repeated measures randomized control group design. *Journal of Autism and Developmental Disorders, 39*(2), 299–321.

Ransford, C., Greenberg, M., Domitrovich, C., Small, M., & Jacobson, L. (2009). The role of teachers' psychological experiences and perceptions of curriculum supports on the implementation of social and emotional learning curriculum. *School Psychology Review, 38*, 510–532.

Rao, P. A., Beidel, D. C., & Murray, M. J. (2008). Social skills interventions for children with Asperger's syndrome or high-functioning autism: A review and recommendations. *Journal of Autism and Developmental Disorders, 38*(2), 353–361.

Rayner, C., Denholm, C., & Sigafoos, J. (2009). Video-based intervention for individuals with autism: Key questions that remain unanswered. *Research in Autism Spectrum Disorders, 3*(2), 291–303.

Reagon, K., & Higbee, T. (2009). Parent implemented script fading to promote play based verbal initiations in children with autism. *Journal of Applied Behavior Analysis, 42*, 659–664.

Reaven, J., Blakeley-Smith, A., Nichols, S., Dasari, M., Flanigan, E., Hepburn, S. (2009). Cognitive-behavioral group treatment for anxiety symptoms in children with high-functioning autism spectrum disorders: A pilot study. *Focus on Autism and Other Developmental Disabilities, 24(1),* 27-37.

Reese, R., Yan, C., Jack, F., & Hayne, H. (2010). Emerging identities: Narrative and self from early childhood to early adolescence. In K. McLean & M. Pasupathi (Eds.), *Narrative development in adolescence: Advancing responsible adolescent development* (pp. 23–44). New York: Springer.

Reichow, B., & Volkmar, F. R. (2010). Social skills interventions for individuals with autism: Evaluation for evidence-based practices within a best evidence synthesis framework. Jo*urnal of Autism & Developmental Disorders, 40*(2), 149-166.

Reis, H., Lin, Y. C., Bennett, M. E., & Nezlek, J. B. (1993). Change and consistency in social participation during early adulthood. *Developmental Psychology, 29*, 633–645.

Resetar, J., & Noell, G. (2008). Evaluating preference assessments for use in the general education population. *Journal of Applied Behavior Analysis, 41*, 447–451.

Rogers, S. J., Hayden, D., Hepburn, S., Charlifue-Smith, R., Hall, T., & Hayes, A. (2006). Teaching young nonverbal children with autism useful speech: a pilot study of the Denver Model and PROMPT interventions. *Journal of Autism & Developmental Disorders, 36*(8), 1007-1024.

Rogers, S. J., & Dawson, G. (2010). *Early start Denver model for young children with autism: Promoting language, learning and engagement.* New York: Guilford.

Rogers, S. J., & Vismara, L. A. (2008). Evidence-based comprehensive treatments for early autism. *Journal of Clinical Child and Adolescent Psychology, 37*(1), 8–38.

Rothman-Fuller, E., Kasari, C., Chamberlain, B., & Locke, L. (2010). Social interventions of children with autism spectrum disorders in elementary school classrooms. *Journal of Child Psychiatry and Psychology, 51*, 1227–1234.

Sansosti, F. J., & Powell-Smith, K. A. (2008). Using computer-presented social stories and video models to increase the social communication skills of children with high-functioning autism spectrum disorders. *Journal of Positive Behavior Interventions, 10*(3), 162–178.

Sarokoff, R. A., Taylor, B., & Poulson, C. L. (2001). Teaching children with autism to engage in conversational exchanges: Script fading with embedded textual stimuli. *Journal of Applied Behavior Analysis, 34*, 81–84.

Satriele, G., Nepo, K., Genter, E., & Glickman, A. (2007). The use of Bluetooth technology to promote independent responding in the community: Reducing the stigma of prompting. http://www.researchautism.org.

Schertz, H., & Odom, S. (2007). Promoting joint attention in toddlers with autism: A parent-mediated developmental model. *Journal of Autism and Developmental Disorders, 37*, 1562–1575.

Schreibman, L. (2000). Intensive behavioral/psychoeducational treatments for autism: Future research directions. *Journal of Autism and Developmental Disorders, 30,* 373–378.

Schultz, R.T., Gauthier, I., Klin, A., Fulbright, R. K., Anderson, A. W., Volkmar, F., Skudlarski P, Lacadie C, Cohen D.J, & Gore, J. C. (2000). Abnormal ventral temporal cortical activity during face discrimination. *Archives of General Psychiatry, 57*(4), 331–340.

Scott-Van Zeeland, A., Dapretto, M., Ghahremani, D., Poldrack, R., & Bookheimer, S. (2010). Reward processing in autism. *Autism Research, 3,* 53–67.

Sherer, M., Pierce, K., Paredes, S., Kisacky, K., Ingersoll, B., & Schreibman, L. (2001). Enhancing conversational skills in children with autism via video technology: Which is better, "self" or "other" as a model. *Behavior Modification, 25*(1), 140–158.

Siegel, B., Vukicevic, J., Elliott, G.R., & Kraemer, H.C. (1989). The use of signal detection theory to assess DSM-III-R criteria for autistic disorder. *Journal of the American Academy of Child and Adolescent Psychiatry, 28*(4), 542–548.

Silver, M., & Oakes, P. (2001). Evaluation of a new computer intervention to teach people with autism or Asperger sundrome to recognize and predict emotions in others. *Autism, 5*(3), 299–316.

Simpson, A., Langone, J., & Ayres, K. (2004). Embedded video and computer based instruction to improve social skills for students with autism. *Education and Training in Developmental Disabilities, 39*(3), 240–252.

Simpson, R., de Boer-Ott, S., & Smith-Myles, B. (2003). Inclusion of learners with autism spectrum disorders in general education settings. *Topics in Language Disorders, 23*(2), 116–133.

Skinner, B. F. (1953). *Science and human behavior.* New York: Free Press.

Smith, T., Buch, G., & Evslin Gamby, T. (2000). Parent-directed, intensive early intervention for children with pervasive developmental disorder. *Research in Developmental Disabilities, 21,* 297–309.

Smith, T., Groen, A., & Wynn, J. (2000). Randomized trial of intensive early intervention for children with pervasive developmental disorders. *American Journal on Mental Retardation, 105*(4), 269–285.

Smith, T., Scahill, L., Dawson, G., Guthrie, D., Lord, C., Odom, S., et al. (2007). Designing research studies on psychosocial interventions in autism. *Journal of Autism and Developmental Disorders, 37,* 354–366.

Sofronoff, K., Attwood, T., Hinton, S., & Levin, I. (2007). A randomized controlled trial of a cognitive behavioural intervention for anger management in children diagnosed with Asperger syndrome. *Journal of Autism and Developmental Disorders, 37,* 1203–1214.

Solomon, M., Goodlin-Jones, B., & Anders, T. (2004). A social adjustment enhancement intervention for high functioning autism, Asperger's syndrome, and pervasive developmental disorder NOS. *Journal of Autism and Developmental Disorders, 34,* 649–668.

Sparrow, S., Cicchetti, D., & Balla, D. (2005). *Vineland adaptive behavior scales: Survey forms manual* (2nd ed.). Minneapolis, MN: NCS Pearson Assessments.

Sparrow, S., Cicchetti, D., & Balla, D. (2006). *Vineland adaptive behavior scales: Teacher rating form manual* (2nd ed.). Minneapolis, MN: NCS Pearson Assessments.

Spence S. (2003). Social skills training with children and young people: Theory, evidence and practice. *Child and Adolescent Mental Health, 8,* 84–96.

Sticher, J., Herzog, M., Visovky, K., Schmidt,C., Randolph, J., Schultz, T., & Gage, N. (2010). Social competence intervention for youth with Asperger syndrome and high functioning autism: An initial investigation. *Journal of Autism and Developmental Disorders, 40,* 1067–1079.

Strain, P., Kohler, F., Storey, K., & Danko, C. (1994). Teaching pre-schoolers with autism to self-monitor their social interactions: An analysis of results in home and school settings. *Journal of Emotional and Behavioral Disorders, 2,* 78–88.

Strain, P., & Schwartz, I. (2001). ABA and the development of social meaningful relations for young children with autism. *Focus on Autism and Other Developmental Disabilities, 16*(2), 120–128.

Strassmeier, W. (1992). Stress amongst teachers of children with mental handicaps. *International Journal of Rehabilitation Research, 15,* 235–239.

Sukhodolsky, D. G., Scahill, L., Gadow, K. D., Arnold, L. E., Aman, M. G., McDougle, C. J., et al. (2008). Parent-rated anxiety symptoms in children with pervasive developmental disorders: Frequency and association with core autism symptoms and cognitive functioning. *Journal of Abnormal Child Psychology, 36*(1), 117–128.

Sussman, F. (1999). *More than words: Helping parents promote communication and social skills in children with autism spectrum disorders.* Toronto: Hanen Early Language Program.

Tager-Flusberg, H., Paul, R., & Lord, C. (2005). Language and communication in autism. In F. R. Volkmar, R. Paul, A. Klin, & D. Cohen (Eds.), *Handbook of autism and pervasive developmental disorders: Diagnosis, development, neurobiology and behavior* (Vol. 1, pp. 335–364). Hoboken, NJ: Wiley.

Tanaka, J., Wolf, J., Klaiman, C., Koenig, K., Cockburn, J., Herlihy, L., et al. (2010). The perception and identification of facial emotions in individuals with Autism spectrum disorders using the *Let's Face It!* Emotion Skills Battery. *Journal of Child Psychology and Psychiatry, 51*, 944–952.

Taylor, B., Hughes, C., Richard, E., Hoch, H., & Coello, A. (2004). Teaching teenagers with autism to seek assistance when lost. *Journal of Applied Behavior Analysis, 37*, 79–82.

Taylor, B., & Levin, L. (1998). Teaching a student with autism to make verbal initiations: Effects of a tactile prompt. *Journal of Applied Behavior Analysis, 31*, 651–654.

Taylor, B., Levin, L., & Jasper, S. (1999). Increasing play-related statements in children with autism toward their siblings: Effects of video modeling. *Journal of Developmental and Physical Disabilities, 11*, 253–264.

Tomanik, S., Harris, G., & Hawkins, J. (2004). The relationship between behaviors exhibited by children with autism and maternal stress. *Journal of Intellectual and Developmental Disability, 29*(1), 16–26.

Tsatsanis, K. (2005). Neuropsychological characteristics in autism and related conditions. In F. R. Volkmar, R. Paul, A. Klin, & D. Cohen (Eds.), *Handbook of autism and pervasive developmental disorders* (3rd ed., Vol. 1, pp. 365–381). Hoboken, NJ: Wiley.

Tse, J., Strulovitch, J., Tagalakis, V., Meng, L., & Fombonne, E. (2007). Social skills training for adolescents with Asperger syndrome and high functioning autism. *Journal of Autism and Developmental Disorders* [serial online], *37*, 1960–1968.

Ventola, P., Levine, M., Tirrell, J., & Tsatsanis, K. (2010). Relationship between executive functioning, autistic symptomatology, and adaptive behavior. Poster presented at the International Meeting for Autism Research, Philadelphia, PA.

Vismara, L. A., & Rogers, S. J. (2010). Behavioral treatments in autism spectrum disorder: What do we know? *Annual Review of Clinical Psychology, 6*, 447–468.

Volkmar, F. R., Carter, A., Sparrow, S., & Cicchetti, D. (1993). Quantifying social development in autism. *Journal of the American Academy of Child and Adolescent Psychiatry, 32*, 627–632.

Volkmar, F. R., Chawarska, K., & Klin, A. (2008). Autism spectrum disorders in infants and toddlers: An introduction. In K. Chawarska, A. Klin, & F.

Volkmar, *Autism spectrum disorders in infants and toddlers: Diagnosis, assessment and treatment* (pp. 1–22). New York: Guilford.

Volkmar, F. R., State, M., & Klin, A. (2009). Autism and autism spectrum disorders: Diagnostic issues for the coming decade. *Journal of Child Psychology and Psychiatry and Allied Disciplines, 50*(1–2), 108–115.

Volkmar, F., & Wiesner, L. (2009). *A Practical Guide to Autism*. Hoboken, N.J.: John Wiley.

Warren, S., Fey, M., Finestock, L., Brady, N., Bredin-Oja, S., & Fleming, K. (2008). A randomized trial of longitudinal effects of low-intensity responsivity education/prelinguistic milieu teaching. *Journal of Speech, Language and Hearing Research, 51*, 451–470.

Webb, B., Miller, S., Pierce, T., Strawser, S., & Jones, W. P. (2004). Effects of social skill instruction for high functioning adolescents with autism spectrum disorders. *Focus on Autism and Other Developmental Disorders, 19*(1), 53–62.

White, S. W., Albano, A. M., Johnson, C. R., Kasari, C., Ollendick, T., Klin, A., et al. (2010). Development of a cognitive-behavioral intervention program to treat anxiety and social deficits in teens with high-functioning autism. *Clinical Child and Family Psychology Review, 13*(1), 77–90.

White, S. W., Keonig, K., & Scahill, L. (2007). Social skills development in children with autism spectrum disorders: A review of the intervention research. *Journal of Autism and Developmental Disorders, 37*, 1858–1868.

White, S.W., Oswald, D., Ollendick, T., & Scahill, L. (2009). Anxiety in children and adolescents with autism spectrum disorders. *Clinical Psychology Review, 29(3)*, 216-229.

White, S. W., & Roberson-Nay, R. (2009). Anxiety, social deficits, and loneliness in youth with autism spectrum disorders. *Journal of Autism and Developmental Disorders, 39*, 1006–1013.

Wichnick, A. M., Vener, S. M., Keating, C., & Poulson, C. L. (2010). The effect of a script-fading procedure on unscripted social initiations and novel utterances among young children with autism. *Research in Autism Spectrum Disorders, 4*, 51–64.

Wichnick, A. M., Vener, S. M., Pyrtek, M., & Poulson, C. L. (2010). The effect of a script-fading procedure on responses to peer initiations among young children with autism. *Research in Autism Spectrum Disorders, 4*, 290–299.

Williams, D., & Happé, F. (2009). Pre-conceptual aspects of self-awareness in autism spectrum disorder: The case of action-monitoring. *Journal of Autism and Developmental Disorders, 39*, 251–259.

Williams, S., Johnson, C., & Sukhodolsky, D. (2005). The role of the school psychologist in the inclusive education of school-age children with autism spectrum disorders. *Journal of School Psychology, 43*, 117–136.

Williams White, S., Koenig, K., & Scahill, L. (2006). Social skills development in children with autism spectrum disorders: A review of the intervention research. *Journal of Autism and Developmental Disorders* [online], December.

Wolfberg, P. (2009). *Play and imagination in children with autism* (2nd ed.). New York: Teachers College Press.

Wolfberg, P., & Schuler, A. (1999). Fostering peer interaction, imaginative play and spontaneous language in children with autism. *Child Language Teaching and Therapy*, 41–52.

Wood, J., Fujii, C., & Renno, P. (2011). Cognitive behavioral therapy in high functioning autism: Review and recommendations for treatment. In B. Reichow, P. Doehring, D. Cicchetti, & F. Volkmar (Eds.), *Evidence-based practices and treatments for children with autism* (pp. 197–230). New York: Springer.

World Health Organization. (1992). *International classification of diseases: Diagnostic criteria for research* (10th ed.). Geneva: Author.

Wright, P., & Wright, P. (2004). *IDEA 2004*. Hartfield, VA: Harbor House Law Press.

Wright, P., & Wright, P. (2007). *Special education law* (2nd ed.). Hartfield, VA: Harbor House Law Press.

Yang, N. K., Schaller, J. L., Huang, T. A., Wang, M. H., & Tsai, S. F. (2003). Enhancing appropriate social behaviors for children with autism in general education classrooms: An analysis of six cases. *Education and Training in Developmental Disabilities, 38*, 405–416.

Yang, T.-R., Wolfberg, P. J., Wu, S.-C., & Hwu, P.-Y. (2003). Supporting children on the autism spectrum in peer play at home and school: Piloting the integrated play groups model in Taiwan. *Autism, 74*, 437–453.

Yingling-Wert, B., & Neisworth, J. (2003). Effects of video self-modeling on spontaneous requesting in children with autism. *Journal of Positive Behavior Interventions, 5*(1), 30–34.

Yirmiya, N., Kasari, C., Sigman, M., & Mundy, P. (1989). Facial expressions of affect in autistic, mentally retarded and normal children. *Journal of Child Psychology and Psychiatry and Allied Disciplines, 30*, 725–735.

Yirmiya, N., Sigman, M. D., Kasari, C., & Mundy, P. (1992). Empathy and cognition in high-functioning children with autism. *Child Development, 63*(1), 150–160.

REFERENCES

Yoder, P., & Stone, W. (2006). Randomized comparison of two communication interventions for preschoolers with autism spectrum disorders. *Journal of Consulting and Clinical Psychology, 74*, 426–435.

Zachor, D. A., Ben-Itzchak, E., Rabinovich, A. L., & Lahat, E. (2007). Change in autism core symptoms with intervention. *Research in Autism Spectrum Disorders, 1*, 304–317.

Zahn-Waxler, C. (2010). Socialization of emotion: Who influences whom and how? *New Directions in Child Development, 128*, 101–109).

Zelazo, P., Qu, L., & Kesek, A. (2010). Hot executive function: Emotion and the development of cognitive control. In S. Calkins & M. Bell (Eds.), *Child development at the intersection of emotion and cognition* (pp. 97–112). Washington, DC: American Psychological Association.

Zercher, C., Hunt, P., Schuler, A., & Webster, J. (2001). Increasing joint attention, play and language through peer supported play. *Autism, 5*, 374–398.

Index